LITTLE LAUREL WINS MONTANA'S BIGGEST BASKETBALL TROPHY

Dennis Gaub

Treasure State Heritage Press
Belgrade, Montana

Treasure State Heritage Press
Belgrade, Montana 59714
win-em-all.dennisgaub.me

Win 'Em All – Little Laurel Wins Montana's Biggest Basketball Trophy/ Dennis Gaub —1st ed.
ISBN-13: 978-1532819803

Contents

Preface

Acknowledgements

First, thanks to Norm Clarke, a fellow Terry, Montana, product who, many years ago, took a teenager who wanted to become a sportswriter under his wings. Also, acknowledgement is due to another Montana small-town guy, fellow Northwestern University journalism grad and premier writer, Ivan Doig, who I first met in the early 1980s and conversed with twice before his passing in 2015. Doig's "This House of Sky" opened my eyes to the possibility of telling stories about coming of age in a special place called Montana. Cheers and big thanks to the 1969 Laurel Locomotives, many of whom shared their priceless memories.

And a special nod to Ric Peterson, who studied the game with the same diligence as his dad, Coach Pete, and is a walking archive of information about the Cinderstellar Locomotives. I extend my sincere appreciation to Dorothy Peterson for giving me insights into a remarkable time that only the wife of a Hall of Fame coach could provide. Credit is due to Roger Seelye's mother, Shirley Seelye, who recorded the 1969 state championship game radio broadcast, allowing it to be shared a half-century later. Alan Campbell deserves appreciation for what he did when he succeeded Don Peterson as coach of the Locomotives: salvaging many items of interest from the 1969 season, including vintage movie footage. Like anyone who loves and earns a living from writing, I acclaim the editing of Craig

Lancaster, a fellow journalist in Billings, Montana. Craig helped smooth out numerous rough patches. Any errors, though, are mine.

Dedication

This book is dedicated, above all, to my wife, Carolyn, and our amazing son, Julian. It would not have been possible without their support and love. You're the best, Gaub Team! As I complete this book, my mind travels back to my childhood in Terry where my late father, William "Bill" Gaub, played small-town high school basketball in the mid-1940s. I remember going to Terrier games with him in elementary school – he and my grandfather, another avid sports fan, took me at an even younger age – and that introduction to sports transformed into a desire to be a sportswriter. During many years of having my byline in the *Billings Gazette*, I doubt there was a more loyal or faithful reader than my dad. Finally, this book is dedicated to the family of Don Peterson, who invited my wife and me to join a Peterson-Sterling family gathering in Billings in August 2014. In my office is a basketball signed by "Team Peterson."

Thanks!

Foreword

In 1968-69, the Laurel, Montana, high school boys basketball team achieved something remarkable. Those 15 purple-and-gold clad Locomotives and their coach, Don Peterson, went through an entire season, 26 games, without a loss and captured the first state basketball championship in school history. The team's final win for the trophy came in overtime on the biggest stage these teenagers had ever played on in their lives.

The Locomotives were undersized all year and faced an even greater height disadvantage going for the trophy. It didn't matter.

They were a small school playing against a larger school, which had happened before. It didn't matter.

A magic season concluded with a magic night that lives on in the memory of players, fellow students, community members and sports fans, all middle-aged now and scattered across Montana and throughout the U.S.; a couple players live or have lived halfway around the world. This book tells the story of how a now-legendary team from Laurel beat the odds to win the state's biggest basketball trophy a half-century ago and became a permanent part of Treasure State sports history.

Why this book now? Thoughts of writing other stories, based on Montana's colorful early 20th century history, ran through my mind at the start of 2013. I was struggling with structuring a book based on one idea when somehow my mind wandered to a piece of history that unfolded before my eyes: Laurel's undefeated run for the 1969 state basketball championship.

By the time I began, a year later, the 45th anniversary of the Locomotives' triumphant night at the Montana State University Fieldhouse was approaching. Newspaper editors — and I'll always be a journalist even if I drew my last pay check as a reporter 20 years ago — love what-happened-on-this-day-(fill in the blank)-years-ago stories. So I contacted my former employer, the *Billings Gazette* and offered a nostalgia piece about the championship game.

Gazette sports editor Mike Zimmer liked my idea and gave me the green light. The article appeared the morning of March 15, 2014 – 45 years to the day after the Laurel-Kalispell title game. To further solidify the bonds between history and now, I sat in the Worthington Arena at the Brick Breeden Fieldhouse (the current name of the MSU Fieldhouse) that same night. I sat next to Jerry Bygren, a starting player for the '69 Locomotives.

Jerry and other Bigfork fans were in Bozeman, cheering for their school's boys basketball team as it pursued and won the first state championship in school history. I had met Jerry, a bank president in Bigfork, a month earlier when I traveled to the northwestern Montana town to interview him. He and his wife, Sarah, hosted me at their home and served me a delicious dinner after Jerry and I traveled down memory lane together.

I was ready to write. I had already tracked down several players from the Laurel team of lore, including star forward Tom Perrigo, in Perth, Australia, and reserve player Dave Brinkel, who was a golf course project manager in Dubai as of 2014. Skype made it possible to interview both far-off Locomotives. Based on those interviews and others of former players closer to home, how could I not write about one of the landmark events in the teenage lives of the Laurel players ... and me, since we're all the same age? This book, their story, is the result.

A life-shaping experience almost a half century ago during my senior year at Billings (Montana) West High School made possible my telling of this story. That was when I started in the profession I loved, and still love, one that sustained me for a quarter century: newspaper reporting.

Thanks to my father's small-town connections, my hometown newspaper hired me as a part-time (weekend) sportswriter, reporting to Clarke, sports editor of the *Gazette*. This job sure beat the heck out of typical jobs available to teenagers in the 1960s such as washing dishes at a fast-food restaurant or even being a paperboy, the term used in that somewhat unenlightened time, for the *Miles City Star*, the afternoon daily newspaper in my previous hometown.

Clarke, several years older than me, was already making a name for himself in sports writing. His career, continuing as a writer for the Associated Press, took him to Cincinnati where he covered the Big Red Machine that dominated major league baseball in the early 1970s and to San Diego to coordinate AP's coverage of the 1984 Los Angeles Olympics. He later broke the story of Denver being awarded the Rockies baseball franchise for the *Rocky Mountain News.* Now, as a man-about-town columnist for the *Las Vegas Review-Journal,* he keeps readers in the know about celebrity deeds and misdeeds in Sin City.

All that lay ahead, though, in September 1968. The memory will never fade of Norm telling me he didn't have enough writers to cover all the high school and college games on a busy Saturday. Could I cover West's high school football game against visiting Kalispell that afternoon? You bet!

That assignment resulted in my first byline in a general-circulation newspaper, though I had written articles for student papers at Custer County High School in Miles City and for West High. The story appeared in the *Gazette* on that Sunday in late September 1968.

On Monday, when I went to school, I sensed myself floating a few inches above the floor. It wasn't an ego trip but rather the sheer thrill of having seen my name above a story in a "real" newspaper. Imagine that. I experienced one of the most exciting things that happened in my 17 years – and the *Gazette* paid me for it.

I sensed I was destined to do this. And Norm continued to cultivate my skills with tips to improve my reporting, skilled editing and offers of opportunity to cover sports events of increasing importance in Billings and in the *Gazette's* sprawling circulation area — the size of New England. A highlight of Norm's mentoring occurred in March 1969 when he invited me to join him and help cover the State Big 32 basketball tournament in Bozeman, Montana. Having a seat at the press table inside the Montana State University Fieldhouse gave me a bird's-eye view of what became the cornerstone chapter in this book.

An education at Northwestern University, which awarded me my journalism degree, enhanced my reporting and writing skills, preparing me for a long, satisfying career in the profession. Those years in the trenches sealed the deal. Being a journalist was my life's calling.

You're invited to come along and soak up the sights and sounds of an amazing season for a group of small-town Montana high school basketball players who won 'em all.

Method

What kind of a book is this?

It's nonfiction, a true account of a successful basketball team. I labored, though, to elevate this above the writing I had been trained for and which appeared beneath hundreds of my bylines in newspapers in four states. My goal was to write a work of narrative journalism, definitions of which abound. (A Google search will bear out my statement.) My simple definition: a book or lengthy piece of journalistic writing that is well-researched and sourced – like any reputable news article – and that tells a good story. And that's true. As a master practitioner of what's often called creative nonfiction puts it, you can't make stuff up.

That premise carries the challenge I faced and imagine anyone else tackling a similar project faces: writing a good, true story that's developed and kept moving by dialogue that's not on hand. I wasn't immersed or embedded, to use current journalistic terms, with the 1969 Locomotives. Heck, we all were 17-year-old high school seniors. Still, I want to show, as much as possible, the story through the eyes of those who experienced it, using scenes and dialogue as tools. I relied on interviews with those who were there – players, coaches and others – along with contemporary news articles. Where I can cite a source for someone's words, you will find them enclosed in quotation marks.

Of necessity, though, I've tried my best to include what might have been said at crucial points in the story. An obvious case involves words similar to those spoken by the most important person in the book, perhaps its protagonist. That is Laurel coach Don Peterson, who died in 2003, long before the idea for this book came to mind. I met Peterson in the 1970s, when I was a sportswriter for the *Billings Gazette,* but any interviews then focused on matters at hand, such as a game just played or the next one on the schedule.

So, with no way to interview Peterson himself, my desire to give a sense of what he might have said required me to rely on others who were there for descriptions of his mannerisms and ways of speaking. In particular, the memories provided by Peterson's oldest son Ric were invaluable.

Asking still-alive and sharp Laurel players to reconstruct what was said during a long season now 45-plus years behind them also was a request difficult, if not impossible, for them to accommodate. Where I reconstructed dialogue, I've showed taking this liberty by putting that conversation (brief) in *italic type,* without quotation marks. I used the same convention to signal what anonymous members of crowds, for example at the state championship game, might have been saying during those high-excitement moments. I hope and trust readers will understand.

I am responsible for any errors in actual or inferred dialogue in the pages that follow.

Introduction

Forty-five seconds remained in overtime of Montana's 1969 State Big 32 basketball championship, matching large Kalispell (both in terms of enrollment, nearly 1,700 students, and lineup size, with a 6-foot-11 center and 6-7 and 6-4 forwards) and little Laurel (slightly more than 400 students and no player taller than 6-2).

The teams, from northwestern Montana (Kalispell) and almost 400 miles away in south-central Montana (Laurel), had battled to a 53-all tie in regulation play.

Cheers from a state-record crowd of almost 11,000 spectators rocked the Montana State University Fieldhouse in Bozeman.

Laurel had edged ahead, 55-54, in the extra period on a pair of Jerry Bygren free throws, and the Locomotives were trying to protect their lead in the seesaw contest.

The stakes were high for Laurel. Don Peterson's crew had swept through regular-season and postseason tournament play. They had won 25 games without a loss and were the Treasure State's only remaining undefeated prep team.

Kalispell's Braves also had a lot to play for. The stage was a repeat of the year before when they had reached the state Big 32 championship game, only to lose to that year's talented small-school team, the Wolf Point Wolves. Would the Braves be bridesmaids again?

Now, a final 26-0 record and the state's biggest championship trophy was on the line for Laurel.

The Locomotives worked their four-corner offense for a last, potential victory-clinching shot in the final minute. The din grew louder. Sparkplug playmaker Alan Campbell fired a pass to fellow guard Lee Perrigo, who at 5-8 was the shortest player on the court and who had jumped center against Kalispell's 6-11 center, Brent Wilson, to start the game.

Perrigo drove towards the basket ...

CHAPTER ONE

A bitter loss but better days ahead?

What a change in mood, among Laurel fans and players, it was that night, compared with the scene on the same floor one year earlier.

At about noon on March 15, 1968, the Laurel Locomotives filed into their locker room at the Montana State University Fieldhouse in Bozeman. That their spirits were sagging would have been obvious to any observer.

"We were 'gutted,'" said Tom Perrigo, a star junior forward on the 1968 Locos squad. Perrigo, a Montana native who grew up in Laurel and has lived in Perth, Australia, since 1975, recollected his and his teammates' feelings in a 2014 email, 46 years after his team's close-as-possible loss, by one point. The outcome sowed continuing controversy.

Coach Don Peterson's squad had absorbed a 56-55 defeat by the powerful Great Falls Bison, an outcome determined by 6-foot-7 senior center and future University of Montana great Ray Howard's tip-in with one second remaining. The Bison and Locomotives were playing a loser-out game at the State Big 32 boys basketball tournament.

A roller-coaster of emotions played out on that fateful Saturday morning.

The loss meant that Laurel, not considered a tournament contender, missed an opportunity to play for the consolation title in the annual event, which brought together the top eight teams from Montana's combined Class AA and A leagues. The Big 32, which existed from 1964 through 1969, grouped schools ranging in enrollment from fewer than 300 students to 2,000 or more (the Billings and Great Falls schools, in cities which also had smaller Catholic schools competing in the league). Laurel, with slightly more than 400 students in its three-grade high school lay at the small end of the enrollment continuum.

It wasn't Indiana's all-class system, which lasted until the 1996-97 season and inspired the movie "Hoosiers," but Montana's Big 32 produced its share of storybook state championships. On this day, however, the Locomotives didn't get to play the role of elated underdog winners.

It's gone into the books as a buzzer-beater victory for the Bison. Peterson, however, didn't see it that way. Neither did other observers in a position to witness the winning play that morning, and they assert to this day that a mistaken call cost the Locomotives the game.

Moments after the game ended, Laurel's veteran coach, a math teacher with a keen analytical mind who was a stickler for the rules, disputed the official's call.

Peterson died in 2003. Based on eyewitness accounts of what happened, though, it's possible to imagine his body language and even get a sense of what he might have said.

Here's the essence of the controversy:

• Did Howard score before the buzzer sounded?

• Did the referee and umpire, likely screened out of a clear view of the backboard, unable to see the overhead clock and unable to hear the buzzer due to crowd noise, wrongly call the basket good?

This scene occurred before precise clocks capable of measuring tenths of a second were standard fixtures at high school gyms and college arenas. Venues in that era also lacked backboards with a feature that's common nowadays: lights mounted around the backboard that flash when time expires, a visual signal that helps overcome the crowd noise that can drown the sound of the buzzer at the end of quarters, halves or games.

Ric Peterson, the coach's eldest son, was a spectator that morning. A high school junior that year and a player on Laurel's junior varsity team who would be a varsity reserve the following season, he watched the game from an upper-level seat. He; his uncle, Emmett Peterson; his mother, Dorothy Peterson; his brothers, Rand, Lon and Rolf; and their sisters, Dee and Lori, sat about halfway down from an overhead catwalk that remains a notable feature of the fieldhouse.

"Seated next to my Uncle Emmett, I honestly thought he was going to charge the floor if he didn't suffer a coronary first," the younger Peterson recalled in 2015.

"We both felt the ball was still in Howard's hands when the clock hit zero. I am confident in my recollection."

Don Peterson expressed his vehement disagreement with the call, according to his son.

"Ray was still in the act of shooting, with the ball in his hand, so the last bucket was too late to count, though dad argued himself blue."[1]

Even if Howard tapped the ball a split-second before the buzzer, the basket should not have counted under existing rules. So imagine what Peterson might have said to the game officials before they dashed off the floor.

No! You can't count that basket. It was a tip-in. He tapped the ball and it fell through the net after the buzzer sounded.

At some point, Peterson, a student of the game, may have reached inside his sport jacket. The pocket contained a well-worn rule book he always carried.

Peterson, his face reddening, may have waved the rule book at the official. As was his wont, he refrained from profanity. But according to Ric Peterson, his father showed his extreme annoyance with anyone, especially a ref who made a call contrary to Peterson's understanding of the rules, in a unique way: his right index finger flexed at the last joint, he would shake his head, give the ref a withering stare and exclaim, "Ah, bull dust."

Peterson probably continued to assert that the rule book said a tip-in is not a controlled shot. Even if Howard had released the ball before the buzzer, the rule said it had to fall through the cylinder before the buzzer sounded to count as a basket.

Peterson might have pointed out that a tip-in was unlike a jump shot in terms of final, split-second legality. Basketball aficionados have seen instances where someone launched a shot just before the

---

[1] The younger Peterson shared his memories of the 1968 game in a text message from Dallas, where he is an optometrist. Peterson joined the Air Force after college, obtained his optometry degree while serving in the military and, following in his father's footsteps as a student of the game, its strategies and rules, coached several service teams.

buzzer sounded and the ball arced into the hoop with zeroes showing on the game clock. And the field goal counted.

Not so here, Peterson might have insisted.

About a dozen of his Locomotive players stood nearby. Some of the younger guys, including juniors Jerry Bygren and Tom Perrigo, reflecting on the scene years later, say they were more interested in trying to catch the eye of attractive cheerleaders. Others, however, probably appeared stunned and shocked. Some may have fought off tears.

The brief drama over, the Laurel squad trudged into the locker room, left to think about the zigzag of events they had taken part in the previous two weeks and to wonder if their momentum had ended.

Even one of the Bison starters that day entertains doubts about whether his talented teammate tapped the ball into the net in time. Mike Houtenon, a senior guard, wonders if his team got a lucky break.

On the opposing side of the discussion, former Great Falls coach Gene Espeland said there's no disputing the legality of the winning basket. He's backed by Tom Wilson, a former Laurel assistant coach who was on the Locomotives' bench that morning. Wilson, who coached the Laurel sophomores that season, remembered watching the late drama as best he could from a limited vantage point. Wilson said it appeared that Howard, the state's top big prep big man, scored a buzzer beater.[2]

---

2 Wilson and his wife moved to Phoenix after retirement. Espeland, whose last coaching stint was at Billings Central in the 1990s, also has retired and spends his winter in Arizona. Espeland, a widower since 2014, returns to Billings in the spring. Two other potential key observers that day, Don Peterson and Howard, are deceased. Peterson quit coaching at Laurel in the late 1970s for health reasons. He and his wife, Dorothy, retired to Bigfork, Montana, a resort community on the shores of Flathead Lake. Peterson briefly came out of retirement to coach Bigfork for a couple reasons, then left coaching for good. He died in 2003 at age 76. Howard became an all-Big Sky player

Here's the most detailed description of the key part of the game, from a March 17, 1968, article in the *Billings Gazette* written by the paper's sports editor, Larry Hitchcock (Clarke's predecessor):

"The Locomotives overcame a 27-21 halftime deficit to grab a 55-52 lead with 1:33 remaining. Great Falls' Chuck Lucero sank a jumper to trim Laurel's lead to 55-54.

"Peterson put his squad into a stall. The tactic worked until the Bison intercepted a pass with 16 seconds left.

"Tom Perrigo fouled Scott Dahmer, sending the Bison player to the free throw line for a one-and-one attempt. Dahmer missed the first shot. Howard grabbed the rebound, batted the ball against the backboard, then dropped it in a split-second before the buzzer. Great Falls won, 56-55."

Controlled shot or not, "the ball had to be airborne before the buzzer to count," said Ric Peterson, who maintains Howard released the ball after the buzzer.

Those who think Howard's tip shouldn't have counted as a basket include one of Ric Peterson's younger brothers, Lon. Somewhat in his quarter, Houtenon, the former Bison player, says his view of how the game ended shifted decades after the event.

---

the University of Montana, where one of his coaches was Jud Heathcote, then a Grizzly assistant. Heathcote later landed the top job at Missoula before being hired by Michigan State University. In East Lansing, he learned lasting fame when his Magic Johnson-led Spartans captured the 1979 NCAA championship. Howard became a physician. After a long and distinguished medical career, he died at age 64 in September 2014 while living in Missoula. In the minds of those who think the Locomotives had a one-point win snatched from them, the argument boils down to two still-unanswered questions: Was Howard's shot in the air before the buzzer sounded? Was a tip-in considered the same kind of shot as a field goal attempt from the floor? That is, if a tip-in were the same as a jump shot or lay-in, the rules then and now state that if a player releases the ball from his or her fingertips before time runs out and the ball falls through the net after the buzzer sounds, the field goal counts. Yet, some of those who continue to discuss the Great Falls-Laurel game believe that rules of that time differentiated between a "controlled" shot and an "uncontrolled" shot. For the former, again using the example of a jumper, a basket counts despite a slight delay between release of the ball and it falling through the net, with the buzzer sounding in between. For the latter, once more using the example of a tip-in, a player must not only release the ball but it must also fall through the net before the buzzer sounds for a basket to count.

Lon Peterson, who refereed high school basketball in Montana for several years (as did his brother, Rand), said he and other officials took part in a mandatory review of the rules before each season began.

He recalled the rules stating that an airborne ball that left a player's hands before the buzzer sounded, and which then dropped through the net, constituted a continuation of a shot and counted as a field goal if it was "controlled" – for example, a jump shot.

A tip-in, however, is not considered a controlled shot under the rules, according to Lon Peterson.

"If it's an uncontrolled shot, it doesn't count" even if a player releases the ball before the buzzer and it goes through the net after time has expired, he said.

Houtenon said he and Don Peterson became "very close friends" after the former Laurel coach retired and he and his wife moved to Montana's Flathead area. "We played a ton of golf together, along with his son Lon and his son Rolf," Houtenon recalled. That camaraderie came naturally for Don Peterson, who also coached Laurel's golf teams, some of which won state championships and had his children on those squads. (His daughter, Dee, played on the 1971 state championship team and his son, Rolf, lettered in golf four years, two of them when the Locomotives won state titles.)

"I have to tell you: Don Peterson was a gentleman. He never talked about the Great Falls-Laurel game" during their later-in-life interactions, Houtenon said.[3]

Not until 2013, a decade after Peterson's passing, did Houtenon get more insight into the Laurel coach's contention that the referees muffed the key call in the 1968 game. His view changed because of a

---

3 Houtenon landed a baseball scholarship to UM. He played for the Grizzlies for two years before the Missoula school dropped the sport. He joined D.A. Davidson and worked for the Montana investment firm for 40 years before retiring in the early 2010s. He lives in Bigfork, where he met Peterson years after sitting on the opposing team's bench during the Saturday morning game in March 1968.

chance conversation with Lon Peterson, who was visiting his mother in Bigfork.

Here's Houtenon's account of the talk: "He (Lon Peterson) said, 'You know, my dad never said this to you; in fact, he said, he told me he never would ... [Don Peterson had a] legitimate bitch about Ray Howard's tip-in. I was a basketball official for 10 years, and I know this to be a fact.' Don made the point to the official shortly after that game was over that, OK, Scott Dahmer was the Great Falls player who went to the free-throw line. I can't remember if it was two shots and he missed one and the second ... (or) if it was one-and-one and he missed the first."

Houtenon recalled the missed free-throw attempt, after which the book took a high bounce and his teammate grabbed the rebound. Howard then tapped the ball into the hoop, but Houtenon says he now thinks it went through the net after time ran out.

Thus what may have happened is that Howard was credited with a basket for a tip-in that was not a shot attempt at the buzzer and thus was not a legal field goal. Houtenon now agrees with the late Laurel coach on that point.

"But the ball bounced high to the left side off the rim and Ray Howard, being the absolute tremendous beast that he was, went up over a Laurel player – no foul involved – but he did indeed tap the ball. It went off the backboard and through the basket. Time ran out while the ball was in the air.

"According to the rule book, a tip is not considered a shot attempt. And Don's contention is the basket should have been disallowed because it was not a legal try for a field goal. Now if Ray had come down with the ball and had possession of it and went back up and it had left his hand before time ran out, and the buzzer rang, that would be, of course, legitimate.

"However, Don's contention to Lon – and Don never told me this, he never in many years even mentioned it – but Lon told me his dad's complaint to the officials was that the tip should not have been considered a shot and therefore the ball going off the glass and time (ending), the ball is going through the basket after the buzzer sounds. And the basket should have been disallowed."

Dorothy Peterson, Don's widow, is in her 80s now, but she retains vivid memories of the contentious finish to the Great Falls-Laurel game.

Interviewed in April 2015, she said:

"I was sitting up in the second tier. The scoreboard was overhead, in the middle of the arena. From the floor, sitting down lower, you could not see the scoreboard and watch the game at the same time – you had to look back and forth."

Her husband, his assistant and the referees all were focused on the action near the basket as time ran out. Given the roar of the crowd, they couldn't rely on hearing the buzzer to know time had expired.

"So it was a big mix-up. Where we were sitting up high, you could look at the scoreboard and watch the game, too. And you saw the (scoreboard) lights (flash) when the buzzer went off."

Dorothy Peterson's voice was firm.

"The ball was still in his hands when the buzzer went off."

Forty-six years and a month after the event, the memories came flooding back as she spoke.

"The reason I remember this when I think about it, and I haven't thought about it for a long time ... Don's brother (Emmett Peterson) was there and we were sitting with him. He just about came totally unglued because we could see it from where we were: that the ball was still in his hand, that he hadn't released it when the buzzer went off."

A small school to be reckoned with

Despite their perennial disadvantage in height compared with most large-school rivals and the smaller pool of potential players to choose from, Peterson's squads had fared well during the five years the league had existed through the 1967-68 school year.

The Locomotives first earned a trip to the state Big 32 tournament in 1966. They gained a repeat trip the following year as divisional champs. Then, in 1968, they made it to the state finals for the third year. Laurel would add a fourth consecutive state tourney berth in 1969. The Locomotives were the only team to achieve the feat of four state Big 32 appearances in the league's brief six-year existence, 1969 being the finale.

After the Great Falls loss, Laurel players were left wondering what might have been. Their season started the first weekend the previous December and was now over in mid-March.

Peterson had guided a young team, led by seniors Bob Crow and Jack Frickel, to third place at the divisional tournament in Great Falls two weeks earlier. Then, because Laurel hadn't already played Livingston, runner-up to the Bison at the divisional tournament, during the tournament, the Locomotives gained the right to challenge the Rangers for a state tournament spot.

Facing a Livingston team led by a future University of Nebraska player, 6-foot-7 Curt LeRossignol[4], the Locomotives came through. They edged the Rangers by one point in the Monday night challenge game. The following week, they packed their bags and boarded the "Grey Ghost," a converted Trailways bus that Peterson (who was also Laurel's athletic director) had acquired. It transported Locomotive athletic teams on long road trips through the nation's fourth-largest but one of its least-populated states. The Locomotives

4 Before his family moved to Livingston, LeRossignol lived in Billings on Avenue C, across the street from Alan Campbell, who later starred at Billings Central. Campbell transferred to Laurel (as described later in the book), and as a senior played a key role in the Locomotives' state championship run. Because of the age difference - LeRossignol graduated from high school a year before Campbell – the two never squared off in a Laurel-Livingston game.

set off for a short 125-mile trek to Bozeman for the state tournament.

Laurel opened play on March 14, 1968, at the cavernous MSU Fieldhouse (which then held almost 11,000 people for basketball games but now seats about 8,300 after a mid-1980s renovation). The Locomotives fell, 47-45, to Butte Central. However, the Locomotives rebounded the next day, whipping the state's biggest school, Billings West – a victory made meaningful by West's proximity to Laurel (about 15 miles apart via Interstate 90).

Laurel's 70-47 thumping of West astounded many, including a telephone operator, who was reported to have said "You must be kidding" when she heard the Laurel-West score. (In that era, a brief delay sometimes occurred while operators connected long-distance calls, allowing them to overhear snippets of conversations.)

The Locomotives' feat was memorable because of what West High had done in its short history. West's doors opened in 1960, and the school graduated its first class in 1962. That year, the Golden Bears began competing in Class AA – then and now the classification for Montana's largest schools, interrupted by the Big 32's six-year existence.

West's administrators, seeking immediate success, especially in what became an intense cross-town rivalry with perennial AA power Billings Senior, hired Red Lodge native Toby Kangas as the school's first basketball coach. Kangas had already made headlines in Montana by guiding Class A Sidney to three consecutive state championships (1957-59). He wasted little time turning the Bears into a top AA competitor. They won the 1963 state AA championship and reached the 1967 Big 32 championship, losing an epic overtime title game to Billings Senior before a capacity crowd in the MSU Fieldhouse.

To make matters more interesting, Kangas was an uncle by marriage to two Laurel players, Tom Perrigo and his cousin, Lee

Perrigo.[5] Frequent social interactions between Tom Perrigo and Kangas were the norm.

"Beating my uncle's team was pretty interesting for me because not only had he wanted me to transfer to West earlier, it (the win) was subject to some interesting family discussions," Perrigo said.

There's no reversing the decisive play or the outcome of the March 1968 Laurel-Great Falls tournament game. An impartial observer also must acknowledge that the game officials called Howard's tip-in as best they could under challenging, confusing circumstances.

Still, Ric Peterson spared no punches as he looked back at the pivotal contest.

"We wuz robbed," he said in an April 2015 text message.

"That '68 team overachieved, like in many other years. Dad always had a strategy in place to counter other teams' strengths and to mask our relative weakness in matchups."

He agreed that the defeat helped motivate him and his teammates the following season.

Asked if the tough loss made the Locomotives an aggrieved bunch going into the 1968-69 season, Peterson said it was not so much that "but a definite expectation to compete well and win most often."

The Locomotives appeared set for another deep postseason run the following year.

"With Perrigo, (Kevin) Flagler, (Roger) Seelye, (Dan) Spoon, Bygren, and a decent supporting cast and experience, Laurel was well-seasoned for the '69 campaign," Peterson said, providing the

---

5Tom Perrigo's father, Harry Perrigo, had played on the all-state basketball champion Billings High team in 1942 when Montana had a two-class system, Class A for the state's largest schools (represented that year by Billings) and Class B (represented by Klein, a now largely deserted former coal mining town near Roundup) for all remaining schools. Chuck Belinak was a star player for Klein. Twenty-seven years later, his son, Mike, was a teammate of Harry Perrigo's son, Tom, on the state champion Laurel Locomotives team.

recollection of someone who became as much a student of the game as his father.

"Perhaps the biggest key was the abundant confidence after the '68 West, Russell, Livingston and Great Falls contests. When Lee (Perrigo) and Soupy (Alan Campbell) transferred to Laurel, the stage was set to compete with all comers in '69."

CHAPTER TWO

A fateful decision sets the stage

"We can't stay here. We're not going to make .500."

Frank Kroll assessed Billings Central's chances of winning at least half its games at a low spot early in his and teammate Alan Campbell's junior year on the Rams' squad.

The Rams kicked off the 1967 season by playing in a tournament at Livingston in early December. They didn't fare well against the host Rangers and Great Falls. In fact, as Kroll said in 2014, recalling what happened more than four decades earlier, "We got pounded."

Soon afterward, several seniors quit the team, he remembered, and Kroll and Campbell talked. First-year coach Dan Burns would return for their senior year at the Catholic high school. Campbell's strained family finances – his father had serious health problems – meant he'd need a basketball scholarship to pay for his college education.

Clouding Campbell's prospects of getting noticed by college recruiters while at Central was football, which appeared to have grabbed the spotlight. The Rams parlayed a solid 1967 team into a state championship the next year when they beat Havre in the Class A title game. (The Big 32 brought Class AA and A schools together only for basketball.)

Kroll had known and played basketball with Campbell since their freshman year. They didn't play together as sophomores because Kroll's parents moved to Seattle so his father could work for Boeing. The family returned to Billings for Kroll's junior year at Central.

Kroll and Campbell scanned Central's basketball roster. It listed good athletes, but by their reckoning they were the only ones who were primarily basketball players. Everyone else seemed to be focused on football with basketball an afterthought.

"I'm not going to get a scholarship out of Central," Kroll remembers Campbell saying. "We need to transfer."

But to where?

Three nearby high schools seemed the best options to improve and showcase their basketball skills: Billings Senior, Billings West and, maybe as a surprise, Laurel, Central's long-time arch rival.

So Campbell and Kroll took an afternoon off from school in March 1968, soon after the state Big 32 tournament had finished in Bozeman, to tour the schools. First, they stopped at Billings Senior, where long-time coach Bill Lazetich had taken the Broncs to the 1967 Big 32 championship. Next, they headed across town to Billings West, where Kangas had built a perennial state title contender. Last, they drove to Laurel.

It's unclear whether Kroll and Campbell spoke to either Lazetich or Kangas. But they agree that they didn't visit with coach Don Peterson during their visit to Laurel. Instead, they conversed with William "Bill" West, the school principal.

Recalling the conversation, Campbell said, "The only question I asked him is would I be eligible to play. He said, 'Sure.' I said, thank you very much. I didn't even talk to Pete (Don Peterson)."

Matters got interesting when they returned to their school for the final period of the day.

"Before we got back, all three people (at the other schools) had called Central. After the last bell, there was an announcement on the PA system," Kroll said.

"Frank Kroll and Alan Campbell – report to the school office," the two friends heard on the speakers.

When they reached the office, the priest serving as school principal got to the point.

"What are you boys doing? Are you thinking of leaving Central?" Kroll remembers being asked.

Kroll said Campbell replied: "We need to go someplace where I can get a scholarship."

Campbell doesn't recall the school office visit as vividly as Kroll, but he agreed that the atmosphere at Central changed for him and his friend that day.

"I don't remember the announcement. I remember when we came back, we went into the office and we kind of got the cold shoulder. We knew something was up. I didn't find out until later that Mr. West phoned Central to find if for some reason we was expelled or kicked out," Campbell said.

"That's all I knew about. We went back to class. From that moment on, we got the cold shoulder. It wasn't very pleasant personally for me the next couple weeks."

Campbell remembers rebukes from a Central teacher and administrator. One frosty moment occurred soon after the school-shopping episode, and it drove Campbell out of Central and to Laurel.

"I was in bookkeeping class. My seat was about in the middle of the classroom, toward the front of the room, and I was doing some work. The teacher was one of the football coaches, an assistant. Pretty good coach, pretty good teacher. I think he was talking about

Central, loyalty and things of this sort. I wasn't paying attention – I was just working.

"All of sudden, I felt everybody had just stopped. I thought maybe he was saying something and I'd better be paying attention. I rose my head, and here he was talking about me. Everybody in the classroom was stunned, stopped or staring at me."

According to Campbell's recollection, the teacher said, " 'A person who doesn't like to be here should just move on. ' The meaning was clear. Evidently he was talking about me," Campbell said, "and everybody else was looking at me."

Campbell got up and left. As he walked toward his locker, the challenge to his loyalty still stinging his ears, he spotted Bob Bryce, his freshman coach, standing outside the door of his classroom. "He was a great guy, a great coach," said Campbell, who was unsure whether Bryce knew what had just happened.

"It wasn't a slamming of the doors, or yelling and screaming. I don't know how and why he was standing out there. He maybe had a premonition.

"I went to my locker, got all my books, and I was so upset at that time I couldn't even stop and say goodbye. That's the one thing I regret, was not being able to thank him (Bryce) for what he did. I walked out and I said I won't ever be back in this place again."

The seed for Campbell's decision to finish his high school education at Laurel was sown earlier, in March 1968, at the State Big 32 tournament in Bozeman. Laurel's eye-catching 70-47 win over Billings West in Friday afternoon loser-out play proved the pivotal event. Its consequences extended beyond the one-upmanship the Locomotives and their followers gained against their big-school peers in Billings.

That's because spectators at the Saturday morning game included two 16-year-olds who were strangers then but would become teammates the following year: Campbell, coming off a season when he won all-state honors as a junior guard at Central, and Ric Peterson, a junior varsity player on the Locomotives squad that year.

Campbell, interviewed 45 years, later remembers the Laurel-West game and how it influenced his life.

"That happened to be the game I watched," he said, discussing his trip from Billings to the Montana State University Fieldhouse. His Central Rams had failed to qualify for the tournament, making Campbell a spectator.

"I was sitting up in the stands, and of course I was kind of in awe because Toby's teams are not like that," he said, surprise still evident as he recalled West's loss. It stunned observers because West's Toby Kangas has been one of the state's top coaches in Sidney before taking the helm at West when the school opened in 1960. Kangas coached the Golden Bears to the state Class AA basketball championship in 1963 and second place in 1964, when the they lost the title game to powerful Missoula Sentinel, which ended that year with a 49-game winning streak and extended it to a still-standing state record 56 games the following season.

"While I was sitting up in the stands, this kid (Ric Peterson) asked me who I was," Campbell said. "He asked me if I was Alan Campbell. I said, 'Yeah.'"

This dialogue between then-strangers followed, as recalled by Campbell.

Peterson: "I heard you're going to transfer."

Campbell: "Yeah, I'm thinking about doing that."

Peterson: "Well, where are you thinking about going?"

Whether he expressed them to Peterson, these thoughts were going through Campbell's mind: "Of course, Laurel was on the floor and West High. I know I had thought about going to West High."

Another option was to transfer to Red Lodge about 60 miles from Billings, where Campbell could join one of his best friends, Tim O'Malley, at the Class B school. They had met as kindergartners in the Billings Catholic school system. O'Malley's family had moved to Red Lodge, so Campbell could have boarded with them and tried to make Red Lodge High School's basketball roster.

Campbell, though, had a light-bulb moment.

"I looked on the floor and I said, Laurel's just down the road, without knowing anything, anybody, any coach, whatever the case might be," he said. Laurel lies just west of Billings along Interstate 90, so it would be easy for Campbell to look after his parents.

Campbell's on-the-spot thinking continued.

"I said to myself, and I told this kid, 'I think I might transfer to Laurel.' And who that was, was Ric Peterson," although Campbell didn't know it at the time.

It didn't take long, though, for Campbell and Peterson to build an athletic relationship that became a lifetime friendship for two men now both living in Texas.

"On the way back to Billings, we stopped at Fry's," a now-closed restaurant in Big Timber famed for its home-cooked food. "Everybody stopped there for hamburgers. We did."

Fate again made its presence known.

"Laurel stopped in there, the team. They were getting hamburgers and stuff. That's when I noticed this kid, Ric Peterson. I say, 'Oh, my God.' Two plus two – Ric and Coach Peterson,' " Campbell said.

He already held a favorable view of Laurel, and Peterson, in spite of the fierce rivalry between his Rams and the Locomotives.

"Laurel always was a good basketball team," Campbell said in 2014, and he recalled a positive moment from his junior year at Central (1967-68). The Locomotives were playing on the Rams' court. Campbell fouled out, and Peterson walked up to him, shook his hand and said, "Good game, Alan."

That compliment replayed in his mind at the 1968 state tournament. "I go, gee whiz, he's a pretty good guy. So that just reinforced my thought about going to Laurel," Campbell said.

He enrolled in Laurel High School on April 1, 1968. Peterson delayed his first conversation with the talented newcomer walking the school halls.

"I was in class for a couple weeks before Pete got hold of me. I think the rumor was ... that I was only going to come to Laurel for a few weeks and transfer back over and play ball for Toby (Kangas) at West.

"Pete got me out of class, I remember, and took me in the back of the gym, the storage shed basically. He asked me point-blank, 'Are you just here for a few months and then are you going to go back and play ball for Billings West?' I said, no sir, if I was good enough and can make the team, I'd really like to play ball here. He just left it at that," Campbell said.

One Locomotive helps another

Fate played a role again in giving Campbell somewhere to live while he got his bearings in Laurel. This time, it had to do with a former Laurel player, Ron Faught, who offered Campbell a spare bedroom at his modest home in the town. The story behind their meeting may have gone something like this:

New guy in town, Ron, and he's a helluva player.

Imagine that possible remark from one of Ron Faught's friends as they warmed up to play adult-level basketball in Laurel.

He's Alan Campbell – you know, the hotshot guard from Billings Central. Remember him, he was all-state last year, the friend might have continued.

Faught had played for Locomotives coach Don Peterson soon after the Cut Bank native took the reins as head man in Laurel at the start of the 1959-60 school year. Faught, who graduated in 1963, logged two years on the roster, giving him an early view of what Peterson would mean to Laurel and Montana high school ball in the coming years.

"Actually, we had a fairly good team my senior year," Faught said. "We were ranked 1 or 2 with Hardin in our division the whole time."

(That year, 1962-63, was the last year Montana used a four-class system – AA, A, B and C – before embarking on the Big 32 setup of combining AA and A schools for basketball play.)

After high school, Faught was hired by one of Laurel's main employers, the Farmers Union Central Exchange oil refinery. The facility, now called the CHS refinery, then and now sits along U.S. Highway 212, the gateway to Yellowstone National Park's northeast entrance over the spectacular Beartooth Highway. Located just north of the highway bridge over the Yellowstone River, the refinery dominates Laurel's skyline and pumps millions of dollars into the local and regional economy.

"I met Al towards the end of his junior year, playing basketball. I was playing city league basketball; I met him through a couple other guys that knew him, that had been playing ball with him in the off-season," Faught said.

Playing basketball on Laurel playgrounds that summer forged a bond between the older but still athletic Faught and Campbell, the high school senior-to-be. It reached the point, Faught said, where Campbell "felt pretty comfortable" asking if he could live at his new friend's house for a while.

"I think he thought things would work out. He had played with some of the kids at Laurel. He knew coming to Laurel, he'd probably be sacrificing some of his stats that he could have had at Central because he had a big junior year," Faught said.

Campbell realized that he'd be joining another all-state player, Tom Perrigo, if he made the Locomotives roster. Faught got the impression that Campbell might have transferred to Billings West, but "I think the reason he picked Laurel was because of Don Peterson."

Faught said that living at his house was an option and he invited Campbell to take a look. "I told him it was gonna be a tight squeeze. He came over and looked at my place," Faught said. " 'Oh, I can live here – I can bunk out,' " Faught recalls Campbell saying.

"He made the decision. We got a small single bed and stuffed it in my utility room. He moved in and he stayed with me. He knew he wasn't going to be able to stay with me the whole year because I was engaged and I was gonna get married in April 1969," Faught said.

A few months into the new school year, Campbell moved out, which Faught said would be better since he was working at the Laurel refinery. "Being in high school, you need to have some supervision from somebody. I wouldn't be around, and it wouldn't be a good idea, you living in my place by yourself," Faught remembers telling Campbell.

Other adults made provisions for Campbell to live with the family of Jerry Bygren, Laurel's starting senior center, an arrangement that lasted through graduation in the spring of 1969.

Faught said he became "really close" to Campbell during his senior year in Laurel. "He looked up to me as a big brother. I never had a brother – I had two sisters – so I looked at Alan as a little brother."

Doing what brothers, biological or surrogate, do, Faught and Campbell agreed about one rite of passage for a high school senior: taking a date to the prom in a snazzy car.

"I had a '68 GTO," Faught said. "Alan wanted to drive that thing. He begged me and begged me to let him use it for the prom. So I let him use it. I think he had pictures taken of him with the car."

CHAPTER 3

A star goes down

As spectators found their seats for the Laurel-Missoula Hellgate game on the first day (March 13) of the 1969 State Big 32 tournament, it's possible to imagine their chatter.

Where is that hotshot guard Laurel had last year? That Kevin Flagler – I think that's his name?

Fans had reason to be on the lookout for Flagler. As a sophomore the previous year, he caught observers' eyes by tossing in 16 points for the Locomotives against Livingston in their 1968 Division One challenge game. In earlier tournament play in Great Falls, he scored eight points against Lewistown and four against Great Falls Russell. News accounts from the 1968 state tournament include incomplete box scores, showing only a handful of double-figure Laurel scorers during the Locomotives' three games. Flagler is not listed, but his play made enough of an impression on sportswriters and sportscasters for them to tab him the top sophomore at the tournament.

Flagler's skills caught the eyes of the editors of *Montana Sports Magazine,* a now-defunct publication that covered Big 32 and Class B high school basketball, Big Sky and Frontier Conference college basketball, and prep wrestling and swimming across the Treasure State.

In their preseason preview of the Big 32 Division I, the magazine's assessment of Laurel said:

"Another standout returnee is 5-9 junior Kevin Flagler. Flagler was among the top three sophomore cagers in Montana last year and has a great future ahead of him."

But as Don Peterson's squad warmed up, Flagler was not on the floor. Why?

Before the school year began, Flagler had suffered an injury that ended the season for him in both sports he starred in, football and basketball. The injury occurred during a practice scrimmage as Laurel's football team prepared for its season opener.

Flagler, who was skilled enough to receive a college football scholarship, was playing his regular position of quarterback for the Laurel varsity squad that late summer day in 1968. Suddenly, his athletic career took a turn for the worse.

"It was a live scrimmage," he said in 2015, recalling what happened. "I was running with the ball, and I got hit high and low from opposite directions. My feet were probably planted in the mud."

Ric Peterson, coach Peterson's eldest son, remembers what happened, prefacing his recollection by calling it a "testament to Kevin's toughness."

"I was the center who snapped the ball before Kevin skipped through the line. One of the Harmon twins – Robert, I think – was the one who hit Kev square on the knee. I heard the pop/crunch near my ear hole as the knee was devastated.

"Kevin didn't want to go to the sidelines, but he was so wobbly we shouldered him off. He watched the rest of practice sitting on the grass."

Neither Flagler nor others on the LHS athletic staff realized the seriousness of the injury.

Flagler visited a doctor. "The diagnosis was if I didn't play football, it would be OK. I did not need surgery, and I would be ready to play basketball. So that's the plan I started," he said.

Flagler sat out the football season. That allowed Lee Perrigo, Tom Perrigo's cousin who had transferred from Worland, Wyoming, to become the Locos' signal-caller for the 1968 season.

When basketball practice started that November, Flagler thought he had healed enough to play. "It wasn't too bad. It was just that it stayed swelled up and sore."

Continued practice brought no improvement; the swelling and soreness lingered. Some insight into the injury that wouldn't heal came early that winter when Montana State University basketball coach Roger Craft brought the Bobcats to Laurel for an exhibition game. Accompanied by MSU athletic trainer Doc Herwig, Craft visited the Locomotives' locker room.

"Coach Pete (Don Peterson) asked if the trainer would look at my knee. He did. He said, 'Well, under the circumstances, I think you need to go see another doctor or a specialist and get another opinion,' " Flagler said.

This time, he saw Perry Berg, a distinguished orthopedic surgeon in Billings (who died in 2004 at age 82). Berg's diagnosis was grim.

"He said there was definitely something wrong. But in those days, there was no arthroscopic surgery. He said, 'We just have to open it up and take a look and see what the problem is.' "

The operation, which required four hours of surgery on Flagler's knee, took place around Thanksgiving 1968.

"He found ligaments that needed sewing up. He took cartilage out. There were bone chips."

Flagler left the hospital with his left knee in a cast. "I was laid up big-time," he said.

That started a regimen of therapy. Flagler returned to basketball practice. He kept working out. The Locomotives kept winning without him in the lineup. They were closing in on a 20-0 regular-season record, with the divisional and state tournaments on the horizon.

Don Peterson's crew now was on the verge of becoming Montana's first undefeated state champions since the mighty Missoula Sentinel Spartans, led by future Duke star and ABA player Mike Lewis, achieved the feat in 1963-64.

One day during practice in February 1969, Peterson pulled Flagler aside.

" 'Well, what do you think? We can put you on the tournament team,' " Flagler recalled his coach saying.

"I said, 'Well, there are 12 seniors on the team. I can play next year – let the seniors play.' " Flagler's unavailability for basketball was part of an unfortunate pattern for Laurel; Don Peterson lost a potential basketball starter to football injuries in 13 straight years at Laurel, according to Rand Peterson, the coach's second-oldest son.

(The Locos used one non-senior down the stretch, sophomore guard Gerry Ready, who contributed clutch points in several games. Perhaps more than Ready's scoring ability, his defensive skills were something that Peterson valued. Ric Peterson said his father, in later years, described Ready as "the best he ever coached running the point in the modulated" defense. A dozen seniors, however, made up the heart of Laurel's championship team.)

Flagler acknowledges that he could have played Laurel's last regular-season game or two and picked up a slot on the tournament team. But a sense of fairness ruled out that option.

Thus, Flagler was a spectator – and an astute observer – when his teammates defeated their first two opponents at the 1969 state tournament and then nipped Kalispell for the final Big 32 championship.

Asked if he can pinpoint the reason for Laurel's storybook season, Flagler paused, then said: "That goes back a long time. There's nothing jumping out at me. I guess in reflection there was just a lot of determination and hustle. Everybody wanted to play ball, and people just hustled and gave it everything they had."

Well before the injury that wiped out football and basketball play his junior year, Flagler heard about the new guy in school: Alan Campbell, the all-state guard at Billings Central who transferred to the Rams' arch-rival school his senior year and became a key component of the championship team.

Flagler said he was pleased to hear Campbell would try to make the roster.

"I'm thinking we're going to have a damned good team. I thought that's great, it's only going to make things better."

While in high school, Flagler made a name for himself in two other sports: track and baseball.

In track, he trailed only Malta standout (and later Olympic hopeful) Craig Stiles in javelin prowess. The two-time state Class A champion in that event (1969 and 1970), Flagler held the Class A record with a throw of 191 feet, 3 inches from 1969 to 1972.

Laurel's American Legion team benefited from having Flagler on the mound. He struck out 14 Miles City batters in a two-hit, 4-0 shutout of the Mavericks on June 13, 1968. The next month, he pitched a no-hitter against Bozeman.

Flagler returned to both Laurel's football and basketball rosters in his senior year, 1969-70. The football season was disappointing; Laurel finished with a 2-6 record, defeating only Glendive and Hardin. In basketball, he and Ready, the only returnee from the state championship team, anchored a Locomotives team that finished second to Whitefish at the state Class A tournament in Billings. Flagler earned second-team all-state honors his final year.

Flagler left for Missoula to attend the University of Montana on a football scholarship. Summarizing his brief career wearing the Griz copper and gold[6], Flagler said: "It wasn't much. I broke my wrist in spring football my freshman year. It was the bone that goes off to the thumb. I was kind of notorious for having bad circulation. It didn't heal."

Through the summer between his freshman and sophomore years, Flagler regularly went to his Billings doctor, Berg.

"I still had the cast on when fall drills started. So, they redshirted me."

Having to wait a year to return to the UM roster proved "very boring," Flagler said. "It wasn't any fun. I was just a very immature, dumb kid, so I quit school."

Ric Peterson said further evidence of Flagler's resilience appeared when basketball practice started in late fall 1968.

"When he started basketball practice with a bulky brace, he was hobbled but outstanding," Peterson said.

But Flagler's toughness had limits.

The Locos ran a lot in practice – "no team was better conditioned," according to Peterson – and their exercise routine included stair running.

"The stairs at each corner were at once brutal and treacherous – especially the down flights. Kevin's cranky knee absorbed an awkward test of the brace going down near where Bernie (Lustig, long time radio announcer for KBMY at Laurel sports events) made his exceptional broadcasts in the gym's northwest corner. Some of us almost wept, and Kevin's rehab was set back even more."

Flagler wasn't the first casualty of the stairs, but he was likely the last.

Referring to his father, Ric Peterson said, "Peterson's Locomotives immediately exchanged the stairs for step-ups and skip ropes. Methinks dozens of knees and ankles are Kevin's beneficiaries."

---

6 UM colors are maroon and silver again.

CHAPTER 4

The run begins

Don Peterson showed little outward emotion – "taciturn" is how his son Ric, one of his closest confidants, recalls his father's bearing.

As the first game of the 1968-69 season approached, however, the veteran coach, in his 10th year at the Locomotives' helm, had reason for concern. Even if he didn't show it, clouds of worry crossed his mind. They sprang from three double-edged swords grasped in his hands.

First, five seniors from Laurel's successful squad the previous year had graduated, although an all-senior group of returnees on the current roster soothed that loss. The returnees included smooth-shooting 6-2 forward Tom Perrigo, who had earned second-team all-state honors the year before when he was one of the top prep scorers in the Treasure State.

Second, the Locomotives might regain the services of Flagler, their 5-9 junior guard who had been a second team all-state selection the year before. Although Flagler had been sidelined for football due to injury, there still was hope that his post-surgery rehabilitation would progress well enough to allow him to play basketball. That hope, though, faded as Flagler's knee showed little sign of healing and he opted to sit out the basketball season.

Peterson faced the pleasant challenge of finding a place in his lineup for two talented newcomers, both transfers: guards Lee Perrigo, from Worland, Wyoming, and Alan Campbell, from Billings Central. Campbell came well-regarded, having earned all-state honors the year before.

Even getting Perrigo and Campbell, though, left Don Peterson apprehensive because of an experience early in his career, when he was coaching a Western Montana high school.

"Lingering was what happened back in Frenchtown when the (Montana) High School Association suspended the school pending the conclusion of an investigation after two top players transferred (into Frenchtown) to play," Ric Peterson recalled. Frenchtown had been a "very strong third-place finisher" at the state tournament the year before, and all its players were returning.

Peterson started coaching at age 19 while still a student at the University of Montana in Missoula. He was so young when he landed his first job at Florence-Carlton that he had to be chaperoned on road trips.

The Cut Bank native's next job was in Frenchtown. (He turned down a chance to be Kangas' assistant in Sidney.) Peterson stayed at Frenchtown, then a Class C and now Class A school, about one year and brought the team far, according to his son.

"They didn't have a lot of talent but they had a couple brothers that were pretty fast and quick," Peterson said. The Broncs also had a couple "big farm boys" who provided front-court muscle.

"He used what they had to really take charge of the conference," and the Broncs became a contender during Don Peterson's time at the helm, Ric Peterson said.

Frenchtown's prospects looked even better the next year, 1950-51, because they played no seniors the previous year and thus had no graduation losses. Players and coaches in the conference gave Frenchtown a good shot at winning the state championship.

The picture only brightened when two players, one from Alberton and the other an all-conference athlete from Arlee, transferred in.

Peterson, though, had already accepted a teaching and coaching job in Belt. His assistant coach took over in Frenchtown, and that's when the state high school association started its probe.

"All extracurriculars got put on hold at Frenchtown while they investigated," Ric Peterson said. What he sardonically called an investigation lasted the entire season.

The Broncs, though favored, were excluded from post-season tournaments because of allegations by superintendents at other schools that the transfers had broken association rules.

The claims were unfounded and Frenchtown was cleared, according to Ric Peterson. He said one transfer had a sister who lived in Frenchtown, and the family of the other transfer may have moved to town.

The memory of what happened early in his career shaped what happened two decades later when talented players Campbell and Lee Perrigo showed up at Laurel. Peterson was wary and still bothered by what he believed was an injustice done to Frenchtown.

"He was spooked," Ric Peterson said. "He wanted to do everything above board. And he had, too, before at Frenchtown, but they got burned," something that bothered Peterson even though he was coaching elsewhere during the investigation.

Peterson was less skittish about Perrigo because he came from Wyoming and was less well-known. Plus, he had family ties in Laurel – a cousin, Tom, on the team, and Lee's aunt and uncle, Tom's parents. Campbell, however, was much more a target of potential suspicion, given he had been an all-stater the year before at Billings

Central and was projected to be one of the top players in Montana as a senior.

"Privately, he may have feared having yet another probable state championship pulled because of transfers and an MHSA probe at the behest of competitors," Ric Peterson said.

This time, though, Peterson's team didn't become the victim of a whispering campaign. Campbell and Perrigo both played key roles in Laurel's undefeated state championship season.

Game week was not when Peterson tended to dwell on what he could not control. It was his manner to apply his analytical mind, the mind of a mathematics and science teacher, to problems at hand – such as how to handle an opponent with respectable credentials.

"Going into the Lovell game at the start of the season, Lovell was highly regarded in Wyoming," Ric Peterson recalled. "They had an all-state guard, John Hoffman. He was very smooth, very fluid, not real fast. He couldn't keep up with Al Campbell. But he was a good shooter, capable defensively."

Peterson briefed his players about the Bulldogs during a "chalk talk" on the Wednesday preceding the Friday night road game.

Guys, he told them, *they have some size inside, so we're going to pressure the ball up front defensively and try to take advantage of their main offensive weakness, which is the lack of a secondary ball handler.*

One of Peterson's players, while absorbing the pre-game strategy from his coach, saw the opening game in a different light than his teammates.

Lee Perrigo hailed from Billings, Montana, where he played grade school basketball and competed in a citywide tournament in which his public school team defeated a Catholic elementary school team on which Campbell played. After Perrigo's father, a Korean War veteran, died, Perrigo's mother moved her children back to where she had grown up and had family, in Worland, Wyoming. Perrigo's athletic career flourished there. He became an all-state football player and a starter for Worland's basketball team.

But Montana beckoned. The presence of family members prompted Lee Perrigo's mother to arrange for him to move to Laurel, live with his father's relatives and finish high school there.

Nowadays, Lee Perrigo says he doesn't remember many specifics about Lovell, although his Worland team had played against the Bulldogs. "We were always supposed to beat them. We were kind of above them (in classification)," he said.

"I know I wanted to have a good game because I started for Worland from when I was a sophomore," Perrigo said. "I think there was some head-scratching" among Lovell players and coaches, who wondered: Is this the same guy we played against last year?

Perrigo, though, ignored the puzzled looks. "At that point, I was trying to earn my starting spot. I just wanted to play well," he said.

He had the advantage, perhaps, of little or no knowledge of – and no preconceptions about – Laurel's opponents for the 1968-69 season. Nor had he realized the talent around him.

"I really didn't know how good we were. I didn't know who we were supposed to win (against) and who were supposed to lose to and who was supposed to be better than us. I just didn't have the history of how good are we. I didn't know how good Laurel was," Perrigo said.

Don Peterson's latest edition of the Locomotives was coming off a 16-win, 12-loss season capped by a drubbing of much bigger Billings West High School at the state Big 32 tournament and a painful loss to Great Falls High that ended the Locomotives' season.

Peterson outlined Laurel's strategy against the Bulldogs at Lovell. *They like to pack into a 2-1-2 or a 2-3 zone defense,* he said. *If we need to, we're going to go into our Mad Dog 1-3-1 half court trap,* he continued.

Although they have one capable guard, John Hoffman, they're a little challenged otherwise when they handle the ball, Peterson said. *They have some size inside, so we're going to try to pressure the ball up front defensively, force the ball out of Hoffman's hands, and try to take advantage of their lack of other ball handlers.*

Peterson, who in 1968 was in his 23rd year of high school coaching, counted on what he considered a fundamental weakness of the Bulldogs.

"One cardinal rule – well, cardinal for my dad – was whoever's bringing the ball up, there always has to be a trailer," Ric Peterson said. "Somebody has to trail behind in case they get trapped or get in trouble. That way you have an outlet."

Lovell didn't follow that principle.

When Hoffman brings the ball up court, we'll press and trap him with two players; he won't have a trailer to pass to, the Laurel coach said. *They're wide open to the trap because Hoffman is their only good ball handler. Make him bring the ball up court every time, with nobody helping.*

Pretty soon, Hoffman will get tired, lose a half step when he drives to the basket and start turning the ball over. That's when the game is lost, Peterson told his team.

On Friday, December 6, 1968, shortly before tip-off, the Locomotives were ready to burst from the visitors' locker room to the floor for final warm-ups. *Wait a minute,* assistant coach Tom Wilson said. *You can't win 'em all if you don't win No. 1.* He had used that motto in his coaching before coming to Laurel, and it became the Locomotives' pre-game mantra for all 26 wins in what former players call "the Cinderstellar season."

Lee Perrigo made the best of his chance to play again in his former home state. He scored 18 points against Lovell, and Laurel's other transfer, Campbell, tossed in 26 to give the pair more than half (44 points) of Laurel's output in the 76-57 win.

The next night, Laurel played again in Wyoming, at Cody, which gave another Locomotives player a homecoming of sorts. Senior forward-center Jerry Bygren had moved with his family to Laurel from Powell, Wyoming, a short distance east of Cody, when Bygren was a high school freshman.

Bygren wasn't happy about the move. Powell had just built a new high school, and its facilities seemed, in the eyes of the teenager, superior to the new locale that his parents had selected.

Bygren, however, adjusted well. By his junior year, he was sharing playing time at center with standout starter Jack Frickel. By his senior year, Bygren was one of the veteran players that Don Peterson counted on. Bygren, rarely a scoring threat but more a presence on the boards, scored five points against Lovell and two against Cody in an 83-63 win.

The opening weekend proved significant for a veteran on Laurel's senior-laden squad, Dan Spoon. Like many youngsters who grew up in Laurel, Spoon played organized basketball in elementary school. Even coaches at that level taught their young charges the basics of Peterson's offensive and defensive plays, starting them on the "Peterson Way" of playing.

As a junior, Spoon made the Locomotives varsity and got playing time on the 1968 team that won a challenge game at the divisional tournament to reach the state tourney in Bozeman.

As his senior year began, Spoon thought his years of practice and game experience – "I worked my ass off," he recalled in 2016 – would pay off and give him a chance to contribute to a Locomotives team already being mentioned among Montana's Big 32 elite.

"I was right there in the mix, like I thought I would be," he said. It became clear, though, that Spoon would mostly sit on the Locos' bench, not start, a disappointment that lingers to this day.

Thinking back, Spoon said he can't remember in which game, Lovell or Cody, a pivotal event occurred, but he still knows what happened.

"They (opposing players) were overplaying Jerry Bygren – back door, fake here, layup. And Lee wasn't getting that. So Pete says to me, 'Go in there," and it's like magic." Laurel's defense stiffened, and the opponents weren't getting easy baskets anymore.

Then, however, Spoon remembers Peterson pulling him out of the lineup and putting Perrigo back in, saying, "Lee, now you know what to do." Spoon had to wonder: "How is this working out?"

Spoon's relationship with his coach deteriorated, but he learned a life lesson. "It was a hugely beneficial time for me because I got to learn how to deal with adversity. But at the time, it was a very unpleasant set of circumstances."

Yet, Spoon's ability to handle adversity, and patience to wait for his moment, would prove crucial later in the year when his heroics at the divisional tournament helped preserve the Locomotives' undefeated season.

The next weekend, after the two-game sweep in Wyoming, Laurel posted win No. 3 at Hardin, beating the fellow Class A Bulldogs, 53-44. The sternest test of the season came next.

CHAPTER 5

Flu and a rugged win

Laurel's biggest scare came in its fourth game, on December 18, 1968, when the Locomotives traveled about 15 miles east on Interstate 90 to face Billings Senior. The Broncs were just one season removed from winning their own state Big 32 championship; they had edged crosstown rival Billings West in overtime for the 1967 crown at the Montana State University Fieldhouse. A near-capacity crowd for that game would be eclipsed by the record throng that watched the Laurel-Kalispell championship game in March 1969.

Laurel notched a March 1968 win over West, which with Senior had the largest enrollment among Montana high schools. A new season with new starters, though, meant the win over West had little bearing on the matchup with Senior.

To complicate matters, there was a big gap in Laurel's lineup for the Wednesday night game. Coach Don Peterson was absent. The veteran head Trainman was home in bed, nursing a case of Hong Kong flu. He listened to the game broadcast, delivered by family friend and the long time Locomotives play-by-play announcer, KBMY's Lustig, Still, Peterson's moderating yet firm guidance was gone when it appeared the Locomotives needed it.

Yet, it wasn't as if Locomotives were left without solid leadership. Peterson turned the coaching reins over to his assistants, Karl Fiske and Tom Wilson. They came through. But they had a rugged experience as they sat in the engineer's chair.

Playing in Senior's outdated "cracker box" gym 7 (long since replaced with a modern facility), Laurel fell behind, 15-1, in the first quarter.

The Locomotives overcame that cold start and outscored the Broncs 18-5 in the second quarter to grab a 30-26 halftime lead. Laurel was up 49-40 with 5:30 remaining when Senior made a run. The Broncs reeled off 12 points to go ahead, 52-49, at the two-minute mark.

Fiske and Wilson realized they had a problem. They called timeout, huddled the Locomotives and tried to impart the right mix of motivation and stern prodding before sending the team back on the floor.

Turning toward senior forward Roger Seelye, Fiske said, *Roger, I want you to play tight defense against Booras.* That might have caused Seelye to wince, or at least to quicken his breathing in apprehension as he anticipated taking on Senior's rugged Greg Booras.

OK, coach, Seelye might have replied. *I'll do the best I can.*

Matters didn't improve. The Broncs "mopped Roger against the end of the gym – they took him out," Ric Peterson recalled. "He was pretty hurt. He blew out his ankle. He was out for weeks, if not a month." Seelye didn't return to action until mid-January.

"It was Booras who took out Seelye," Peterson said.

"When the game got rough, Billings Senior got rough, too," Peterson said.

---

7 Allan Olson, who played basketball for Billings High School in 1943 and was interviewed in 2016, recollected that players quickly learned about the gym, which along with the school, opened three years earlier. A low pipe made shooting from one corner an exercise in futility because unless a shot took a flat trajectory, the ball was certain to hit the pipe.

"They put me in. I went into the three position in the shuffle. I gave him (Booras) the jab step and went around him."

Peterson, a senior reserve, said he was "no speed merchant. You had to time me in the 100 with a calendar."

"But I got around Booras," he said. "He lowered the boom. He hit me in the head with his elbow."

Peterson said he was "seeing birds and hearing bells," so someone led him to the free-throw line to attempt two shots for being fouled while shooting.

"I banked one in, but I couldn't see the hoop. He hit me so hard I'm sure I got a concussion out of it, and I don't remember the rest of the game," Peterson said. He sat out the remainder of the game.

Fortunately, the Locomotives could answer muscle with clutch shooting in the late going. Fiske sent in a stalwart from his football team, Mark Metzger, who came through in the clutch.

The Broncs were still ahead, 54-51, with 1:35 remaining, but Laurel's press turned the tide. The Locomotives capitalized on Senior turnovers – the home team had 27 – to rally. Two Tom Perrigo free throws gave Laurel the lead for good, 55-54, with 45 seconds left. Then, Metzger iced the win by sinking two free throws with 23 seconds left.

Years later, he recalled being unsure of how important his shots would become.

"When I shot those two free throws, I glanced up at the (scoreboard). We were ahead. I thought there's no real pressure on me. I shot the two and made them," he said.

He realized, though, that Laurel held a precarious 57-54 lead with enough time remaining for Senior to go ahead.

"They could have come down and done something but they didn't," he said.

In fact, the Broncs did. Dan Pekich sank a 20-footer – there was no three-point arc then – with six seconds left to close the margin to one. There it stayed when the buzzer sounded. Laurel had a 57-56 win and might have lost without Metzger's free throws.

Metzger still appreciates his coach's ability to meld a team from individuals with excellent basketball skills while minimizing egos.

"Peterson actually set us down, maybe it was (preseason) practice or our first game when we had our starting five. He said, 'I've got 10 ball players, 12 ball players.' And he said, "Probably any of you could go start for another team.'

"He said, 'Do you guys want to be a really good team?' " If so, Peterson continued, he'd need to make tough decisions about who to start. Metzger knew he and others wouldn't get the minutes that Laurel's top five players would.

But that didn't cause resentment. "Don Peterson was very fair. If he thought it was your time, that you'd be the best against this defensive person, you'd be in there," Metzger said.

Peterson repeated the team theme throughout the season, and Metzger became a lifetime believer.

"He wasn't my best friend, but I respected him like you couldn't believe. I didn't get a whole bunch of playing time, but you knew when he put you in there, you were in to do a job."

CHAPTER 6

A superfan checks out the Locomotives

Recovered from the flu, Don Peterson returned to his teaching and coaching duties at Laurel High School in time for the Locomotives' last game before the 1968 Christmas break.

Great job, fellows, he might've said to his assistants, Karl Fiske and Tom Wilson.

Still, showing a small smile, he might have added, *could you guys have made it easier on a sick man?*

The Locomotives were coming off a one-point Wednesday night win – their closest of an undefeated season – over always-powerful Billing Senior. Though he wasn't on the bench but bedridden at home, Peterson must have felt the tension since he was listening to a radio broadcast of the game.

All in all, a nail biter. Let's hope we don't have too many of those this year, Peterson may have said.

Now, let's get ready for Friday night. Win that one, and we'll have some momentum going into the new year.

Most Locomotive fans got their first look at the 1968-69 squad when it played host to Lewistown on December 20, 1968.

Excitement already was building about what some fans – most of them cautiously, a few brashly – were saying could be Peterson's finest team in his 10 years at the LHS helm. Maybe this would be the breakout year when the Locomotives won the first state basketball championship in school history.

The Locomotives gathered around their coaches in the locker room for final instructions. In what was becoming a theme, they heard Wilson say:

Guys, you can't win 'em all if you don't win number five. Go get 'em!, coaches and players responded.

The Locomotives burst out of the locker room and ran onto the floor. A packed gym greeted them with a roar of delight. Fans were already amped by hearing the school pep band's rendition of "Sweet Georgia Brown" and the Locomotives' trademark song, "I've Been Working On The Railroad."

I've been working on the railroad
All the live long day
I've been working on the railroad
Just to pass the time away
Can't you hear the whistle blowing
Rise up so early in the morn
Don't you hear the captain shouting?
Dinah, blow your horn

To the delight of the crowd, home fans and visiting fans alike, the Locomotives had warmed up earlier with moves borrowed from the Harlem Globetrotters, another tradition instilled by Peterson.

Those awaiting tip-off included one of the Locomotives' most loyal fans, a self-described "sports nut." Edie Thompson had come to the Laurel gym unaccompanied by her husband – his loss, she said, recalling the evening more than 45 years later.

Mrs. Thompson saw the Locomotives cruise past Lewistown's Golden Eagles, 66-49. The Trainmen led at all quarter stops, 19-10, 37-27, and 46-33.

Alan Campbell paced Laurel with 19 points, and two teammates also reached double figures: Tom Perrigo, 17, and Jerry Bygren, 14. That balanced attack helped compensate for the absence of Roger Seelye, out for a month due to an injury he sustained in the Billings Senior game.

When Mrs. Thompson returned home, she spoke to her husband, Art, who owned the local Farmers Union Insurance agency.

"I said, 'You really should go to these games. This is a special team,' which they turned out to be."

"He went and never missed another (home) game," Mrs. Thompson said of her husband, who died in 2001. The Thompsons were good friends with Don Peterson and his wife, Dorothy. That may have led to Art Thompson volunteering to run the clock at Laurel games.

"We always teased him (Art Thompson). We said Don got him to do it so he wasn't booing in the stands," Mrs. Thompson said.

Her husband, though, had learned of Mrs. Thompson's passion for high school sports years before. "When we got engaged, he had to wait until I got out of a basketball game because I've always been a sports nut," she said.

Her husband's passing hasn't slowed down Mrs. Thompson. "I've always gone to games. In fact, I still go to most of them even though I'm old.," she said in March 2016 when she was 83.

CHAPTER 7

Locos stay united during a town strike

As 1969 began, the Locomotives' play hinted at good things to come. Don Peterson's squad had won its first five games of the season. Yet, January 1969 presented a different test of the team's character, something off the court and away from school that had the potential of dividing the team as it divided the town.

On January 5, what became a 25-day strike began at Laurel's oil refinery, on the east side of town. Other than the railroad yards, nothing anchors Laurel's economy like the refinery. That was so in 1969 when the Farmers Union facility employed about 150 workers. It remains so now. The industrial facility, now called CHS and much larger after major expansion projects in 2008 and 2014 (with another project underway in 2016), employs about 300 people year-round and has a workforce that reaches 500 when contractors are added. It is the largest taxpayer in Yellowstone County.

The strike was part of a nationwide work stoppage by the Oil, Chemical and Atomic Workers International Union. Main issues were wages, job classifications and fringe benefits.

The strike began the day after the Locomotives defeated Hardin, 56-34, to boost their record to 7-0. Laurel started the year with a 53-42 win over visiting Miles City.

About 600 members of Montana locals of the OCAWIU, seeking a pay increase of 72 cents an hour over two years, walked off the job. Besides the Farmers Union refinery in Laurel, facilities affected by the strike were:

- The Continental Oil Company of Billings (now a Conoco refinery).
- The Humble Oil Company of Billings (now an Exxon refinery).
- The Phillips Petroleum Company of Great Falls (now Calumet Montana Refining).
- The Big West Oil Company of Montana at Kevin (now defunct).
- Union Oil Company of Cut Bank (now defunct).

Executives at the Laurel, Billings and Great Falls plants said they would continue operating while workers were on strike. They planned to use management personnel to keep refineries operating.

Almost immediately, hints of an ugly dispute appeared. On January 6, 1969, on the second day of the strike, a spokesman for the Laurel local of the union told a reporter that management had brought in strike-breakers – scabs – to staff the plant. A union spokesman said that two carloads of men crossed the picket line. Officials at Farmer's Union headquarters in St. Paul, Minnesota, confirmed that managerial personnel from the main office had been sent to Laurel to help keep the refinery operating. Meanwhile, one day into the strike, the chairman of the union's Laurel local said that the work stoppage probably had already cost union members more than the raises they were seeking would bring them in a year.

The Locomotives basketball team, however, bridged the divide because it had players with parents and friends among both strikers and management.

Recalling the strike, Leon Schmidt, a top reserve on the championship team whose father died when Leon was 13, said his connection to the strike was through his uncle, Jake Schmidt, a blue-collar worker at the refinery.

"It went on for quite a while, and it was cold," Schmidt recalled. Still, touches of civility and community surfaced amidst the acrimony, he said. "If I recall, for the white-collar workers (who continued working inside the plant), they brought in freezers and put in meat and stuff like that."

Schmidt singled out the decency extended to Tom Perrigo's father, Harry, who was among those isolated inside the refinery.

"I really think the community got together – the union and (management) and said, 'Look, Harry Perrigo, you're not going to miss your son's game. We're going to let you cross the union line to see your son play.' That's my understanding: that the union got together and said this is too important."

Asked about that, Tom Perrigo, who has lived in Australia for four decades, said he couldn't recall his father discussing that aspect of the strike before he died years ago. He said his father, a star player on the Billings High School all-class state championship team of 1942 and later a starter for then-Montana State College's football team, talked more about football.

Someone else with first-hand knowledge of the strike, Ron Faught, looks back at the dispute from multiple perspectives:

- As someone who played basketball for the Locomotives on a pair of Don Peterson's early Laurel teams (1962, 1963).
- As someone who, after leaving high school, continued playing basketball in pickup games and thus got to know Alan Campbell the first summer he spent in Laurel and even let the boy room with him.
- As a white-collar employee of Farmers Union who worked in a refinery office.

Faught recalled being locked inside the refinery after the strike began. "I was working on the same shift and in fact in the same unit as Harry Perrigo. We were working the night shift together. We were listening to the ball games on the radio (while handling operational tasks normally done by workers picketing outside)."

Teammates Mike Belinak and Jerry Bygren had parents in contrasting roles during the strike. Belinak's father, Chuck, an operator at the refinery, was on the picket line. Bygren's mother worked in the refinery's purchasing department, which was moved across the highway from the plant during the strike. Staffers in that department worked regular daytime shifts, unaffected by the strike.

Another person found himself in an unclear situation during the strike. That was the father of Gary Whitney, a younger player on the junior varsity in 1968-69 who would play on Laurel's 1970 and 1971 State Class A runner-up teams. Faught said Whitney's father was a union member but had been promoted to a management position at about that time. Faught was unsure when the promotion took effect, before the strike or afterward. So Whitney's father may have been a shift foreman working inside the refinery, or still an operator carrying a sign outside.

Faught juggled dual loyalties during and after the strike because he was engaged to a daughter of Albert Ehrlick, who was an operator and among those picketing outside the refinery. Ehrlick's son, Darrell, was a sharp-shooting star of the 1967 Locomotives basketball team.

"So I'm on the inside and my future father-in-law is on the outside, making turkey tracks that they throw out. He was a welder, and he made those turkey tracks that were like 2-inch things where no matter where you threw them on the ground, there was a point sticking up. They'd throw 'em out there for the drivers bringing trucks into the plant so they could flatten the tires."

The *Billings Gazette* reported on January 15, 1969, that negotiations appeared to be at a stalemate, quoting the Laurel union leader as saying a 35-minute negotiating session the previous week resulted in no offer to negotiate any specific issue and no plans for further talks.

"Their parting remark was, 'Don't call us, we'll call you,' and we're puzzled by the reluctance on the part of the company in this area to begin any type of meaningful negotiations," said union leader Leo Yeager (who also was a high school basketball official and took part in pre-season clinics to brief the Locomotives on rules changes).

The brief meeting with Laurel workers was the only one in the area that week; strikers and management at the Continental and Humble refineries in Billings did not confer. Meanwhile, settlement talks in the nationwide strike had begun in California.

On January 15, 1969, the *Gazette* published a large ad, paid for by Farmers Union, detailing the company's position in the dispute.

Finally, on January 30, 1969, the strike ended. Laurel refinery workers won a two-year contract that included a 65.6-cent hourly wage package, job classification adjustments, higher shift differential and improvements in fringe benefits such as health insurance and early retirement pay.

Meanwhile, the Locomotives kept rolling. Starting with their wins over Hardin and Miles City at the beginning of the month, they ended January 1969 with a 14-0 record. Other wins were at Glendive, 60-50; at Sidney, 82-66; against Great Falls Central, 60-44; at Bozeman, 74-45; against Glendive, 70-41; against Sidney, 81-60; and at Lewistown, 56-53.

CHAPTER 8

A scare in Lewistown

Whether they were superstitious, Laurel players couldn't help wondering: Was No. 13 bad luck?

On January 25, 1969, the Locomotives validated their new No. 2 ranking in the state Big 32 (Class AA-A) power poll by whipping visiting Sidney, 81-60, to push their record to 13-0. Depth? The Locomotives proved they had it. Eleven Laurel players scored, led by Tom Perrigo with 17 points. Alan Campbell added 16, Roger Seelye 12 and Jerry Bygren 11. Guard Gerry Ready, brought up from the sophomore squad, hinted at good things to come by scoring four points.

Too short to control the boards, with no one taller than 6-2? Not a problem that Friday night. The Locomotives built a 62-33 rebounding margin.

But this triskaidekaphobia thing – the anxiety that keeps airlines from having a 13th row and tall buildings from having a 13th floor – might have seemed to have a delayed effect about 24 hours later.

The Locomotives traveled to Lewistown the next day (January 31, 1969) to play a Golden Eagles squad they defeated, 66-49, at home in their last game before the 1968 Christmas break.

In the teams' second encounter, Laurel grabbed a 15-8 first-quarter lead that proved no security. Lewistown rallied for a 28-all tie at halftime, and the score stayed knotted at 37 starting the fourth quarter. Matters became interesting and worrisome. Let Bygren, the Locomotives' steady senior forward/center, describe it:

"We were down by about eight points with about three minutes to go," he said, when Coach Don Peterson called time out.

We're going to our press, Peterson told his players, who had learned to sense and share the veteran coach's confidence in that defensive tactic. The Locomotives went to their 3-1-1 defense, the fabled UCLA 7/8ths court matchup devised by Bruins' coach John Wooden.

Peterson instructed his tallest players to stake positions in front, their arms in the air, and he positioned cat-quick senior guard Alan Campbell as "The Gambler" in the middle of the defensive set. Front-line Locomotives threw their arms high, trying to generate lob passes, while in the backcourt, Lee Perrigo tried to stop the ball handler if Lewistown broke the press. The resulting delay would allow teammates to fly back into a half-court defense.

"He (Peterson) always put the best anticipator in that middle spot. He'd concede they're going to make that pass and you're going to beat the ball there. And that's what Al was so good at," Bygren said.

"We ended up winning that game by three or four points. We slapped the press on; Campbell stole the ball a couple times, Tom (Perrigo) had a steal, and maybe Lee (Perrigo). They couldn't hardly get the ball in bounded.

"Wham, wham, wham. All of sudden the game was tied and then we went on to win," Bygren said.

Bygren spotted his adoptive parents in the crowd. "I remember standing at the free-throw line and looking at my mom and dad in the stands, just sort of shaking my head, thinking it's getting a little tight. And Pete called that timeout right after the free throw and said, 'OK, we're going to press. I want you to press hard and get your hands in the air.' "

Tom Perrigo and Campbell together scored 12 of Laurel's 16 points in the fourth quarter, and the Locomotives secured a 56-53 win, No. 14.

It was, Laurel players agreed as they looked back years later, one of their two most challenging regular-season games, the other being the win at Billings Senior.

"I think those two games were confidence-building," proof that the Locomotives could win on the road in unfriendly surroundings, Bygren said.

CHAPTER 9

Lassoing the Cowboys

Imagine the mixture of pride and apprehension percolating through the Grey Ghost, the nickname for Laurel's team bus, as driver Larry Leatherman piloted the converted Trailways coach toward the Eastern Montana town of Miles City.

Don Peterson and his Locomotives got a couple days to digest the news: their 17-0 record earned them the No. 1 ranking in the state Class AA-A power poll. Montana's sportswriters and sportscasters voted unanimously to name Laurel the top team in the Big 32 that week.

Now, the 160-mile drive, largely on two-lane U.S. Highway 10/212 (Interstate 90 was uncompleted), took the Locos to their first test of their exalted status.

Awaiting them were the Custer County High School Cowboys, coached by veteran mentor Bob "Pappy" Nees. Nees already had two state championships to his credit. He, like Peterson, would be voted into the Montana Coaches Hall of Fame.

The Cowboys won't be a pushover by any means, Peterson and his assistant coaches cautioned their players as the bus traveled east.

Just think back a couple years, another coach might have added. In 1967, Miles City traveled to Billings for a two-game series against big-city rivals Billings Senior and Billings West. The Cowboys nipped Bill Lazetich's Senior squad inside the Broncs' antiquated and confining gym on Friday night. They traveled across town on Saturday to play in the Golden Bears' lair, a gym that in less than a decade since its doors opened had become one of the most intimidating venues in the state. The Cowboys narrowly lost to the Bears.

No one knew back in the winter of 1967 that West and Senior were on a collision course for supremacy. That March, they squared off for the state Big 32 championship at the MSU Fieldhouse in Bozeman. Senior, led by future Stanford football All-American and NFL player Pete Lazetich, topped Toby Kangas' squad in overtime in front of one of the biggest crowds to ever watch a basketball game in Montana.

The Cowboys had a proud basketball tradition beside which the Locos' legacy paled. Miles City, playing in Montana's big-school ranks until 1950, had won six state championships through 1969. That total trailed only Butte (9), Helena (8), and Billings Senior (7).

Miles City also finished second at state three times. So the 1969 Cowboys only had to look at trophy cases in the halls of the school or talk to community elders to appreciate the tradition they were expected to continue.

Laurel, meanwhile, had never won or played for a state basketball championship going into the 1968-69 season.

It's easy to imagine Alan Campbell, an easy-going people person, walking the aisle of the Grey Ghost, telling his teammates a "Pappy" anecdote to loosen them up.

You know that Pappy, he always has silver dollars in his hands. He rubs them together for good luck, Campbell might have told his teammates.

To relax on the trip, Campbell walked to the back of the bus and played a board game or cards. Sometimes Monopoly pitted Campbell against Don Peterson on a table the coach had mounted inside the vehicle. Campbell usually ended up with more cash, Peterson with more property.

Just as often, though, the Laurel coach took on his players, team managers and other coaches in the game of Tickertape, which taught investment strategies. When Campbell played, he excelled at increasing the value of his Campbell Soup stocks. The Locomotive contingent also liked Canasta and Gin Rummy, played for a penny a point.

(Don Peterson always was the game scorekeeper; he carried lists of what he was owed in his wallet. At his 2003 funeral in Bigfork, Montana, his son, Lon, who operates the family ranch near Cut Bank, Montana, wrote a check on the ranch account for the full amount owed his father. The check accompanied Don Peterson to his internment in Cut Bank. Lon Peterson's parting advice was, "Dad, don't spend it all in one place.")

Pop and rock music of the period also floated through the Grey Ghost on this and other trips. The bus logged close to 3,000 miles crisscrossing central and eastern Montana during the 1968-69 season. Campbell functioned as disc jockey at the back of the bus. Using a play list built by classmate and school newspaper photographer Art Armstrong, the Locomotives grooved to songs such "I Can't Get No ... Satisfaction" (Rolling Stones), "Dizzy" (Tommy Roe), "This Magic Moment" (Jay and The Americans), "You've Made Me So Very Happy" (Blood Sweat and Tears) and "Let the Sun Shine In" (5th Dimension).

Once the bus got to Miles City, the Locomotives faced a long wait before their game.

"I remember there was like three games we had to sit through and watch," Campbell said. "They had the freshman game, B squad and JV game. By the time our game came along, we were all tired."

The Locos, however, got a burst of adrenaline when they walked onto the floor.

"The Miles City cheerleaders had basketball uniforms on. We've never seen anything like that – that kind of made us do a little high-stepping," Campbell said.

Laurel got a further lift from something else intended to motivate the Cowboys.

"We were warming up, and Miles City had a pep band. They were up on the stage playing 'Wipeout' and this kind of stuff that was the music I had played to in my backyard (while growing up in Billings)," Campbell said. (The CCHS band, one of the best in the state, included the author's cousin, a member of the percussion section.)

"There was about three or four of us. Ric Peterson went up and dunked the ball. (Jerry) Bygren dunked the ball

"I was the last one. I couldn't get up there with one hand so I dunked the ball with both hands," Campbell said.

At the time, dunks were permitted in warm ups but not during games under Montana high school rules, patterned after the so-called "Lew Alcindor rule." When Jerry Bygren broke a backboard with a dunk before a game in the divisional tournament at Great Falls Russell, causing a long delay, Laurel coaches discouraged dunks during warm ups.

The game with Miles City started, and Laurel raced to an 8-0 lead in the first 40 seconds, Campbell recalled.

Nees called a timeout to regroup. Campbell, who made friends everywhere he went, strolled over to chat with Randy Spear, a senior guard for the Cowboys.

Campbell said he told his opponent, " 'Randy, you better tell that band to stop. This thing isn't going to get any better if they don't.' The band didn't play after that."

Still, it was a rugged contest. Miles City was called for 17 fouls; Laurel was whistled for nine personals.

The win became a trademark outing for Metzger, a senior reserve on the team. Metzger was known for his all-around toughness – he wasn't tall nor did he weigh a lot. Still, newcomers to Laurel Junior High School, trying to find their place in the adolescent hierarchy, learned to not tangle with Metzger, according to Ric Peterson.

Recalling the game in 2014, Metzger said, "Miles City was really hands-on, hands on our backs the whole game.

"Lee Perrigo was in first. He couldn't do much – try to run through and a Miles City player would push him out."

So Don Peterson sent in Spoon, another reserve from his senior-laden squad.

"Danny went in for a little bit. He couldn't do anything," Metzger said.

"Coach (Karl) Fiske says, 'Put in Metzger – they ain't going to push him around.' "

Fiske, Peterson's top assistant, also was Laurel's head football coach and had Metzger on his squad the previous fall.

"I was the same size then as now, about 5-8, 165. I was a middle linebacker on the football team. I wouldn't say I was the toughest guy in the class, but I wouldn't take any crap, either.

"One of the Miles City guys had his hands on me. I kind of pushed my way through. I said, 'Get your hands off me.' He said, 'Man, what are you going to do?'

"We went on. We came down with the ball the next time. We set up our offense and I went to cut through. The kid was pushing on me again, so I just brought up my fist and dropped him. I don't know who it was to this day."

Matters got hectic. Laurel turned over the ball. The referees apparently didn't see Metzger's uppercut. They were the only ones who missed it inside the packed CCHS gym.

"I didn't get a foul. They picked up the ball and came to their end. The (Miles City) kid was laying on the floor, and they called timeout. The stands were going nuts.

"Oh, yeah, everybody saw it. Next thing I know I'm sitting on the bench. Peterson's chewing my butt. 'What the hell did you do that for? You're done.' "

At least one coach, however, appreciated Metzger's action.

"Ole Fiske, he pats me on the back (and says), 'Good job. They ain't going to have their hands on you for a while,' " Metzger said.

Now playing without Metzger, the Locomotives stayed on track. They defeated the Cowboys, 56-53, and ran their record to 18-0.

Campbell led the Locos with 23 points, Tom Perrigo scored 20, and Bygren added six.

It wasn't the first time that Metzger tangled with an opponent that year. Ric Peterson recalled the eighth game of the season, on January 10, 1969, when Laurel visited Glendive. There, Metzger laid "one of the biggest hits I ever saw" on a Glendive guard. "Mark planted a blind pick and relieved the Red Devil of his teeth. I saw a couple of good shots in other games, but that one still sticks in my mind," Peterson said.

One hundred sixty miles away, back in Laurel, the night proved enjoyable for two faithful followers of the Locomotives, Dorothy Peterson, Don's wife, and "Punky" Graham, wife of another LHS teacher and coach, Bob Graham.

Mrs. Peterson was born and started growing up in Iowa. She got a chance to play high school basketball, and that began her lifelong love of the game. Then, her family moved to Cut Bank, Montana, where she finished high school and met her future husband.

She attended most Laurel boys basketball games at home and on the road. On the night of February 14, 1969, however, she stayed in Laurel and watched a movie with Punky Graham, wife of Laurel teacher and coach Bob Graham. While keeping an eye on the screen, the two listened to the game on earphone-equipped transistor radios.

As Mrs. Peterson listened, she got the sense she had heard the radio color guy before, likely in a broadcast during the 1960-61 season. There's no way of knowing for sure, but it possibly was Gordy Spear, editor of the Miles City Star and father of Cowboys player Randy Spear. And just as had happened eight years earlier, the Miles City color guy said little positive about the undefeated Locomotives.

"The announcer – I'll never forget – he said, 'I don't see what they brag about this Laurel team. They don't show me anything special. They don't even have a star.' "

That announcer didn't realize his accurate analysis helped explain the success of the role-playing, no-place-for-stars Locomotives.

CHAPTER 10

No Campbell Soup for the Rams

Laurel Locomotives players and fans elevated one team on their schedule above the others from the late 1950s on, and so it was in 1969. They accorded and still accord arch-rival status to Billings Central, the Catholic high school located 15 miles away near the downtown of Montana's largest city.

Stories circulate of Laurel visiting the "old" Central gym (since renovated and expanded and now known as the Ralph Nelles Center in honor of one of the private school's main donors) and being greeted by the sound of low overhead pipes clanging as zealous Ram fans banged on them. Central got an equally hostile reception when it visited the Locos' court.

The 1969 Laurel-Billings Central games, though, took on special significance in the schools' long rivalry. That's because 5-10 senior guard Alan Campbell was a starter for the Locomotives. Central partisans knew him well. He had advanced through the Catholic school system in Billings, played pickup ball in the driveway of his family's home on Avenue C and earned a spot in the Rams' starting lineup. He earned all-state honors wearing the green and white as a junior in the 1968 season, when many observers considered him one of the state's top guards and a certain college prospect.

Then, for personal reasons and without being recruited, Campbell left Central after the season ended in March. By early April 1968, he had transferred to Laurel.

Some intense feelings were inevitable, but they appeared to have been muted when Laurel defeated visiting Central, 74-64, in the team's first meeting in early February 1969. Accounts of the game indicate nothing noteworthy other than the play on the floor.

Hot-shooting Central cut the lead to four points in the fourth quarter before Laurel's Tom Perrigo combined a layup and two free throws to give his team a comfortable 70-60 lead. Perrigo finished with 23 points, Jerry Bygren got 17, and Campbell added 13. Campbell and Perrigo sparked a ball-hawking defense that caused 22 Rams turnovers; Laurel had 13. Laurel also owned the boards, with a 51-29 edge in rebounds.

That victory made Laurel 16-0. The Locomotives advanced to 17-0 the following Saturday night with a 68-47 triumph over visiting Bozeman. The following Monday, the Locomotives awoke to news they had been voted No. 1 in the state Class AA-A power poll, the first time they topped the Big 32 that year.

Coach Pete's squad protected its ranking with two road victories the next weekend: 59-53 over Miles City and 61-50 over Livingston.

Laurel now needed just one win to own a 20-0 regular-season record and to go into divisional and state tournament play with a chance of becoming Montana's first undefeated state champion in five years. The last obstacle to a perfect regular-season record, appropriately, was Billings Central on the Rams' floor

Expecting an overflow crowd that would require turning away disappointed spectators, Central officials moved the February 22 game to Billings West's larger gym.

That's when Campbell tasted the acrimony his departure from Central had caused.

"Yeah, I remember it very clearly," Campbell (known to some of his friends as "Soup" or "Soupy") said in a 2014 interview while living in Texas, his home for more than 20 years.

"I can't put a few things in words, but it was discouraging to me in some (respects). I guess I came to the realization that some of these people don't like me.

"I remember we walked into the West High place, which I've always wanted to play in, and about the only things I saw were signs on the wall (with drawings of) Campbell Soup with bullet holes in them. Tomato soup running down. And blood (symbolic) running down.

"It was kind of a death warrant, is how I looked at it," said Campbell, now in his 60s, recalling his shock as a 17-year-old at the sight of vitriol directed against him.

"We warmed up. It was a packed house. I remember going in for layups, underneath there were several young kids. They were yelling, 'traitor' at me and this and that. That kind of got to me."

Hey, one of the Locomotives yelled during warmups, *there's a hot spot in the floor. Let's do some dunkin'*. A supple spot on the left side of the basket gave balls and players extra lift.

That started what players recall as a "dunk fest" during their five-line warmup. Many of the Rams watched. Central owned the crowd, but it's possible Laurel's eye-catching pregame routine tempered some of the animosity directed at Campbell by students and fans of his former school.

As usual, the Locos threw the UCLA 3-1-1 matchup zone against the Rams. Still, the game was not a breeze, especially for Campbell.

He remembers his coach calling timeout a couple of minutes into the game. "I started walking off to the other end of the floor. They rattled my bones so damned bad that I didn't even know where I was at that time."

The game attracted a sell-out crowd of 3,100. They saw the Locos build a 16-point lead, 66-50, with 2:49 left. This was after the Rams closed to eight points in the fourth quarter. Then Laurel's disciplined offense and Central's inability to convert free-throw attempts sealed the outcome, a 71-62 Laurel triumph.

Seelye poured in 22 points to pace Laurel. Tom Perrigo, despite being double-teamed, got 17 points, all in the first half. Foul trouble hampered him in the second half, and he picked up his fifth personal with a little more than five minutes left in the game. Bygren, turning in one of his top efforts of the season, scored 15.

Displaying their trademark accuracy at the free-throw line, the Locos canned 23 of 29 attempts, and 17 of 19 after intermission. Central went 13 of 23.

Although Campbell scored five points, well below his season average, he again was a one-man press breaker, displaying quickness and foot speed unmatched in the state. He alone doomed Central's defense, a man-to-man half-court press, and he threaded passes to Bygren for easy bunny shots. The Rams double-teamed Tom Perrigo, but that set Seelye free to can basket after basket, using a smooth left-handed jump shot that got raves everywhere Laurel played.

For Campbell, the game represented a triumph in other ways than the outcome.

Peterson pulled him for a few minutes in the second half. Central used its press to make a run and seemed to have momentum. So, Peterson sent Campbell back into the game, and he broke the press and got the ball up court.

Campbell has not forgotten what happened later.

"After the game, (assistant coach) Karl Fiske came out, grabbed me on the floor and said, 'You're a Locomotive now.' That meant a lot to me because I wasn't born and raised there. I didn't come up through the system and try to be like everybody else."

Campbell said it was "fortunate" that the Locomotives won what was "not a very enjoyable game for me."

CHAPTER 11

Stolen shoes and glory in Great Falls

The Grey Ghost, Laurel's beloved if quirky team bus, pulled off Highway 89 and onto Sixth Avenue, the main business arterial in Great Falls, then Montana's largest city but soon to be surpassed by Billings.

Don Peterson had bargained for and converted the used Trailways coach into the vehicle that transported his basketball teams and other Laurel athletic squads on long road trips across the state. The bus was reliable, although stories still circulate of it stopping running for no apparent reason and then starting up again on its own.

Driver Walt Parker, who shared behind-the-wheel duties with Larry Leatherman, piloted the bus into a parking spot alongside the Midtown Motel, where the Locomotives stayed during the Big 32 Division 2 tournament and which had a café where the team ate all but two meals during the three-day event. It was February 27, 1969, and the top-ranked Locomotives were heading to the Great Falls Russell High School Fieldhouse and their opening-round game. As players spilled out of the bus, someone noticed a box with copies of the *Great Falls Tribune* for sale.

Wonder what the Trib has to say about us?, one player may have asked others. Someone fished coins out of his pocket, paid for the morning paper, pulled out the sports section and read out loud to the rest of the Laurel contingent.

"Laurel comes into the tourney with an enviable 18-0 conference record and the regular season conference championship," *Tribune* sports editor Mayo Ashley's column began. "Not since 1964 has a major high school team in Montana rolled up an unbeaten record and it is truly something to be proud of." The Locomotives boasted a 20-0 season record, including the non-conference wins over Lovell and Cody, at that point.

Hey, I like that, one player said to his peers. His mood, though, changed as his teammate continued reading.

"However, one gets the feeling, looking at the schedule, that Laurel is not all that overpowering. Nowadays, to win in the tough Big 32, a team has to have a little break from the schedule. Laurel had it this year just as Kalispell did one year ago when it won the league crown," Ashley wrote.

Oh, no, groaned someone in the small knot of boys as they moved toward the cafe door. *He's comparing us to Kalispell; they played second fiddle to Wolf Point last year, and you wanna bet he thinks we're gonna come up short this year, too?*

Ashley's column noted that Laurel defeated only one team that finished in the Big 32's Top 10 ranks that season: Billings Senior. The Locomotives notched six wins against the league's middle 10 teams, and the other 11 victories came at the expense of the Big 32's bottom dozen teams, Ashley pointed out.

"This is not to downgrade a fine record by a fine team. It is merely to point out that the Locomotives are not all powerful as the record would indicate," he wrote, complimenting Peterson's coaching job. He pronounced Laurel the favorite "but don't expect a waltz."

Yet, the Locomotives couldn't avoid thinking Ashley said that the host Rustlers stood a good chance of ending Laurel's long winning streak. After all, the Rustlers had won three of four games against teams in the Big 32's Top 10 and had split four games against the middle echelon. Russell had duplicated Laurel's success against the bottom dozen teams, picking up 11 victories.

We'll show that guy, one of the Locomotives vowed as the waitress led them to their table.

Ron Faught also sensed that Laurel wasn't getting the respect it deserved as the divisional approached. He was an experienced basketball player, having played on Peterson's 1962 and 1963 teams that battled Hardin for Class A divisional honors just before the Big 32 came into existence. Faught stayed a loyal Locomotives fan through the years after high school and was among an estimated 2,000 backers who braved the 200-mile drive on two-lane winter roads to the tournament in Great Falls in late February 1969.

"There was a lot of talk and speculation going on – sure, Laurel was unbeaten but they haven't played the bigger teams, big-school teams," he recalled.

Perhaps joining the damning-with-faint-praise crowd, Great Falls Russell coach Doug Palmer told a reporter that Laurel hadn't played a tough schedule. Yet, he said, "Nobody's got to them yet."

The Locomotives made their divisional tournament debut against Great Falls Central and cruised to an 80-49 win, No. 21. After a tie at 19, the Locomotives reeled off 17 straight points to take the lead for good. The Mustangs tried a man-to-man defense, but they couldn't stop Campbell's cut in the shuffle. He slipped through the Mustangs' defense for five layups, finished with a game-high 20 points and set up other baskets with his precision passing.

Three of his teammates also reached double figures: Bygren, 17 points; Tom Perrigo, 16; and Spoon, 11.

The victory sent the Locomotives into the semifinals against Lewistown. The Golden Eagles had given the Locomotives a scare in the regular season, falling by three points on the Lewistown court. In that game, Laurel had to rally from an eight-point deficit in the fourth quarter.

The tournament was different. The Locos' 3-1-1 matchup press stymied Lewistown, which resulted in key steals. Laurel's took advantage of the Golden Eagles' 2-1-2 zone for wide open shots, causing Don Peterson to later say the contest was "like shooting fish in a rain barrel." Dominant rebounding rounded out an overpowering performance; the Locomotives led at all the quarter stops and won going away.

Scoring honors went to Seelye, who tallied 20 points with deadly shooting. Bygren added 15, and Tom Perrigo had 13. Campbell scored nine points, dipping below his season-average double-figure production, but he dazzled the Eagles and the crowd with his passing and defense.

Pressure was building on Laurel. Bozeman Holy Rosary, in Montana's Class C ranks, had gone undefeated in 19 games but then stumbled and lost in divisional tournament play. That left the Locomotives, now 22-0, as the Treasure State's lone undefeated squad. A divisional championship showdown against Great Falls Russell awaited Pete's squad.

Meanwhile, CMR whipped Billings Central, 102-65, in their divisional semifinal game, setting a school scoring record. Russell fans asserted that Laurel would become their team's next victim. "I'll bet the Laurel players will be shaking in their beds," one was reported to have said in the Gazette.

Campbell remembers the lack of respect that greeted the Locomotives before and upon their arrival in Great Falls.

"They kind of all said we weren't playing anybody," he said. The win over Billings Senior? Well, the Broncs, after winning the 1967 state championship, were suffering through a subpar season.

"Every week, it was, 'Are these guys that good?' I remember going to Great Falls, and Great Falls (Russell) had a good team with Sparky Kottke," Campbell said. Consensus among sportswriters and sportscasters seemed to be that Russell, led by all-state guard Kottke, was talented enough to knock the Locomotives off the top rung of the Big 32 ladder.

Memories of a pre-game meal before the championship clash remain vivid in Campbell's mind.

The team gathered in a conference room. Peterson passed around newspaper clippings. The articles said "that we hadn't played anybody, and this was going to be a butt-kicking time. That motivated us to play as good as we did," Campbell said.

Campbell said he and his teammates respected the Rustlers as a good team. Responding to people who say to this day that Russell should have won, Campbell says, "that's probably a hallmark of our team – a lot of teams probably could have beat us, but no one did. "

Besides the outcome, the game became memorable to Campbell because he had to play in borrowed shoes. And not just any shoes. Shoes loaned by the opposing team's star player, Kottke.

"Our tennis shoes were stolen before the game – well, my tennis shoes. We suited up for the game, and I can't find my tennis shoes," Campbell said.

He had left his shoes in the sweat room/drying room where uniforms were hung to air out because they would get used three or four times in as many days during the tournament. Those shoes were not just regular basketball shoes of the time but the trend-setting Adidas in which Peterson had outfitted the Locomotives.

Someone walked off with the fashionable footwear worn by Campbell and the other Locos. Player recollections state that everyone's Adidas were lifted.

What am I gonna do? Campbell asked Peterson.

Let me see. Maybe we can borrow some shoes, his coach replied.

It turned out that the only player there who might have a shoe size that matched Campbell's was fellow guard Kottke.

"So I got his practice shoes, those Chuck Taylor high-tops. They were broken in. I said, 'I'll use these. I was born and raised in these.' So he let me use his shoes," Campbell said.

As the teams warmed up, Campbell approached Kottke.

"I said, Sparky, these shoes are really good. I appreciate it. They will make my feet pretty happy today."

Ric Peterson's recollection of the event parallels Campbell's. "The whole team's shoes got lifted," he said, adding that locker rooms at the CMR gym weren't monitored by a concierge-like person, as they were when tournaments were played at Laurel's gym. Thus, the team didn't notice the heist until they went to their dressing room.

"We were the only team in the state with Adidas because my dad made special arrangements to get 'em. They took 'em all."

Peterson, a 6-1 senior, wore shoes lent by Ted Ackerman, Russell's 6-1 junior forward – someone with the same height and similar build. Campbell and Kottke, though, were dissimilar. Kottke was a husky all-state tailback in football, too, while the slender Campbell concentrated on basketball. Fortunately, their feet were the same size.

A turn-away crowd of 5,500 packed the CMR Fieldhouse to watch the divisional championship game. Spectators saw what looked like an easy Laurel win before the Rustlers rallied to set the stage for late heroics by a pair of unlikely Locomotive players.

Laurel led, 22-8, after one quarter. The Locomotives went up, 31-12, on Campbell's basket with 2:10 left in the half, and they remained ahead by 16, 33-17, at intermission.

The Trainmen controlled the tempo in the third quarter, building a 17-point lead on Campbell's reverse layup. Laurel still led, 45-34, starting the fourth quarter.

Then CMR made its run. The Rustlers twice closed the gap to three points. Meanwhile, three Laurel starters, cousins Lee and Tom Perrigo and Jerry Bygren, fouled out, as did Russell's center, Larry Landsverk.

That left it to sophomore Gerry Ready and senior reserve Dan Spoon to save win No. 23 and Laurel's undefeated season. Ready sank two free throws, and Spoon, who finished with 11 points, canned a crucial field goal and converted two free-throw attempts down the stretch.

Afterward, Peterson admitted to worrying when the Rustlers cut the gap to three points. He told *Billings Gazette* sportswriter Hudson Willse: "There was a little anxiety, but when Ready canned the two free throws (giving Laurel a 47-42 lead with 2:42 left), I knew we were in because the kids were handling the ball well.

"It wasn't that Russell was doing anything to get back in the ball game. We were just missing too many close shots. We lost our board strength and we had to go to the control game at that time," he said.

The Rustlers, Peterson said, "are real fine shooters. I'm not taking anything away from them, but they weren't able to get the shots against us."

Although Peterson didn't say it, others think the overflow crowd on Russell's court gave the home team even more advantage by influencing the officials. Still, there's no denying that Russell was an excellent team, with a solid offense and good size and speed, the latter exemplified by Kottke.

The comeback kid

For Spoon, the game represented a redemption. He had grown up in Laurel and had played organized basketball since his elementary school days. He recalled spending much of his free time playing pickup basketball against older kids at the nearby junior high school gym, which was an escape from a "hugely dysfunctional" home life.

Spoon got varsity playing time as a junior on the 1968 Laurel team that reached the State Big 32 tournament. So after working hard to master Peterson's complicated defensive schemes and his offensive playbook over the years, Spoon thought he had a shot at lots of playing time, maybe even starting, as a senior.

Those hopes were dashed by the arrival of talented transfers, Campbell and Lee Perrigo. Spoon mostly rode the bench. As he said in 2016, his relationship with Peterson deteriorated. His minutes dwindled. Something else slipped away, too.

"Basketball is all about confidence, and I lost my confidence and played tentatively," he said looking back on the championship season.

Here's how Spoon remembers the divisional championship game.

"We were homered," he said, referring to Laurel's loss of three starters on fouls. "They (CMR) just said, 'You're going to have to beat us with your second group,' and we did."

Spoon, who later lived in Great Falls, competed against Kottke in high school and played with him in city league basketball. "He was an awesome player. Right before halftime (of the championship game), he turned his back on me. I stole the ball and laid it up."

The buzzer, however, had sounded, so Spoon's layup didn't count. Still, "the whole locker room was on fire," he said.

The Locomotives needed every bit of that fire, combined with the steady leadership of Tom Perrigo, to pull out the close win. Thinking of the atmosphere after Perrigo fouled out, Spoon said, "He was so positive. He wasn't going to play (but) he wasn't sitting back (and saying), 'Well, I'm out of here. You aren't any good without me.' He was instrumental in making sure that the energy was there."

If Spoon thought his confidence was gone, it came back when Laurel's lineup was depleted in the fourth quarter. "That's why I played well at CMR. There was nobody else," he said.

Spoon realized that with no one available to replace him, "It's yours. I'm not going to get taken out."

After Spoon and Ready's clutch play made possible the 52-47 Laurel win, something else happened that caused Spoon to have lasting respect for Perrigo. Recalling the ceremonial net-cutting ceremony to celebrate the win, Spoon said, "That's the beauty of Tom Perrigo. When this (divisional championship) happens, he puts the net around me."

Spoon said Perrigo told him, " 'Dan, you're the one.' That's why you give this guy credit. He's not out there going, but for me. He's going, 'You did this. Thank you.' That's the way he is."

And those shoes Campbell borrowed from Kottke? "I kept on kidding him through the game," Campbell said. "I said, 'God, I really like these shoes, Sparky – can I keep 'em?' We got a good laugh out of that. I gave him his shoes back after the game. I don't know if I would have been able to play unless Sparky lent me his practice shoes."

Triumphant return

On the Sunday following the divisional championship, the Locomotives returned to Laurel aboard the Grey Ghost as a caravan of cars with horns blaring escorted the bus into town and to the high school parking lot. There, several hundred people waited. Jubilant fans surrounded the team on a cold afternoon. A banner, "Welcome Home State Champions," waved in the breeze. The sentiments were premature, but no one cared. Laurel boasted the only undefeated team in the state, a squad that had already defied the odds for the second time in three years by winning the divisional championship with a short but scrappy lineup.

"I think some of the things we read in the newspaper up there helped us. They said we played too easy a schedule," said one player, reviewing what had happened since Thursday in Great Falls. Another said, "You might say we didn't like what we read."

Peterson told a reporter that the ingredients for Laurel's success remained unchanged: defense, team pride and unselfishness. Two players pointed to other complementary factors. Tom Perrigo pointed to the one-point win at Billings Senior back in December as what got the Locomotives started. Campbell, finishing his first and only full year at LHS, said team unity gave the Locomotives the edge over opponents. "Nobody cares who gets the most points on this team. It's the kind of team everybody dreams they could play on," he said.

Expanding on his comments as an adult in his mid-60s, Campbell said in 2016: "I came to Laurel knowing that I was on someone else's turf and it was up to me to fit in with the Locomotives' system and students rather than them adjusting to me."

Willse summarized how the "experts" had been proven wrong – again – in a March 2, 1969 article headlined "Laurel Makes Some Believers."

"At Great Falls, they were saying that Locomotives had played a weak schedule, that Great Falls Russell's scrappy man-(to)-man defense would dominate the championship game and that the Rustlers would win by at least 10 points," Willse wrote.

"They even doubted the ability of guard Lee Perrigo and the Locomotives' reserve strength. But Perrigo's skeptics must have cringed a bit when he drove around Russell's highly-touted Warren Kottke for three easy baskets in the first period of Saturday night's championship game," he continued.

Russell's overpowering 37-point victory over Billings Central in the semifinals provided more evidence for those not sold on the Locomotives, who noted that Laurel had defeated its arch-rival by more modest 10- and 11-point margins earlier in the year.

So, the purportedly tougher CMR schedule, which included the Rustlers' win over defending state champion Wolf Point, made it appear to some that Laurel's undefeated run was a "myth" destined to crumble in the post-season, Willse wrote.

"The one thing that they didn't take a close enough look at was the Locomotives' harassing and very effective defense, which along with the tremendous play of Campbell and fine efforts by the reserves, spelled the difference against Russell," he said.

Other congratulations poured in: telegrams from several hundred Laurelites who hadn't been able to attend the divisional tournament; from Montana Governor Forrest Anderson; from Billings Mayor Willard Fraser; from restaurateurs and businesses the Locomotives patronized; from Don Peterson's University of Montana fraternity brothers; and others. Players who remember that congratulatory tide, and who now are part of the Internet age, say today's congratulatory text messages and emails do not carry the same prestige that a Western Union telegram did in their high school days.

Now, with 23 consecutive wins, the Locomotives could set their sights on becoming Montana's first undefeated state Big 32 champions since the 1964 Missoula Spartans.

CHAPTER 12

All set for the big stage in Bozeman

Twelve Locomotive players tried to keep their adrenaline in check soon after daybreak on Thursday, March 13, 1969. They boarded the Grey Ghost, its heat turned up on a chilly, late-winter morning. Don Peterson and his assistant coaches, Karl Fiske and Tom Wilson, joined the bundled-up, Bozeman-bound contingent.

So did the Locomotives' cheerleaders: Sally Smith, the sole senior, and her fellow spirit sparkplugs, Sheri Muri, Claudia Turcotte, Marlene Sonstegaard and Patti Ann Daley.

Can you believe it?, someone might have asked. *We're going to state and nobody's got a better record than us.* A possible reply: *Yeah, but there are some good teams coming this year. Hope it's a happy trip home this time, not a bummer like last year.*

It took the Locomotives about 2½ hours to make the 130-mile trip on a wintry two-lane highway most of the way. The team had a quick light lunch at the restaurant in the Topper Motel, which was their tournament headquarters.

The Topper, a landmark for decades on North 7th Avenue, was "out of the way in a quiet area of Bozeman," Ric Peterson recalled. "Also, the restaurant met my dad's rather high-quality food criteria. We dined well and at strictly controlled intervals to ensure we were ready at game time."

Then the Locomotives headed to the Montana State University Fieldhouse, the biggest basketball arena the younger players had ever seen. At about 1 p.m., a dozen purple-and-gold-clad players burst out of the locker room and ran up the walkways from the fieldhouse's dirt base to the raised, portable parquet floor originally used to switch from rodeo to basketball competition at the arena. They warmed up for the tournament-opening game at 1:30 against Missoula Hellgate, runner-up to Kalispell in the Big 32's Division Four.

The Knights made a respectable early showing, grabbing an 8-0 lead and holding a 14-9 edge at the end of the first quarter. Then, Tom Perrigo showed his leadership. With slightly less than three minutes remaining in the first half, the Laurel all-stater converted a three-point play, and the Locomotives grabbed the lead for good.

They stretched a 26-23 halftime margin to 48-30 after three quarters. By game's end, the Locos had canned a state-record 35 free throws (on 45 attempts), and they romped to a 71-47 victory.

The outcome allayed Peterson's early worries. "I was beginning to wonder when the shots were going to start dropping," he told *Billings Gazette* sports editor Norm Clarke afterward.

When the game became one-sided, Peterson sent in substitutes. *Let 'em rest up for Friday night. No need to chance an injury now,* he said.

Campbell joined the exit. He came off the floor and sat at the end of the team bench.

About then, the Great Falls Russell team walked by. The Rustlers were paired with Anaconda in the 7:30 game that evening. They had watched Laurel's win and wanted to see some of the second game, Wolf Point against Butte Central.

Campbell noticed Sparky (Warren) Kottke in the group of Rustlers. Kottke had loaned his practice shoes to Campbell two weeks earlier at the divisional tournament when the worn by the Locomotives were stolen from a room where uniforms were hung to dry.

"Spark, how ya doing?" Campbell said to his benefactor. Kottke and a teammate or two came over, knelt by the bench and chatted with the personable Laurel star.

Campbell put his hands in the air as he told a story. A *Great Falls Tribune* photographer spotted the group and thought it might make a good image. He snapped a photo of Campbell, Kottke and the others, which appeared in the Tribune the next morning.

The caption for the photo said Campbell was telling the Rustlers a fish story. But that wasn't so.

"I really think I was telling them about the majorettes' boobs," Campbell said, chuckling as he recalled the conversation among hormone-driven teenage boys.

Thinking about how he and Kottke, fierce competitors on the CMR floor in a close game earlier that month, sized up each other's skills, Campbell said, "Because he let me use his shoes, we got a pretty good respect for one another. He didn't think I was an a-hole, and I didn't think he was an a-hole. He was a pretty good ballplayer."

Game Two of the tournament surprised many sportswriters, sportscasters and others who had followed the Big 32 that winter. Butte Central's Maroons defeated the defending state champ Wolves, 46-40. That ensured a new Big 32 champion for every year of the league's existence, six as of 1968-69. The upset also erased the possibility of an envisioned dream game: Wolf Point, which in 1968 came from the smaller Class A ranks and won the state title by beating Kalispell, versus the up-and-coming Laurel Locomotives, also from the Class A ranks, hoping to achieve the same feat.

The Maroons would face Laurel in the Friday night semifinals. For the Locomotives, the big challenge would be slowing down the Maroon's high-scoring guard, Joe Antonietti, who won the Big 32 regular-season scoring title with a 24.7 points per game average.

Having a different matchup than the so-called experts had deemed likely didn't seem to matter to the fans. A state record basketball crowd of 10,700 people packed the fieldhouse to see if the Mining City club could halt the Trainmen. The previous record was set 11 years earlier during the first year the fieldhouse was open. That 1958 crowd came to see the then-Montana State College Bobcats play the Elgin Baylor-led Seattle University Chieftans (now called the Redhawks). Baylor led Seattle to the NCAA championship game that season – his team lost to Kentucky – and then went on to NBA stardom.

Peterson's squad wasn't at 100 percent strength against the Maroons. Bygren was battling strep throat; after the game, the senior center was bussed back to the Topper rather than to the team dinner. Senior forward Tom Perrigo showed up with flu-like symptoms. Fortunately, the rock-solid community and parental support included two key people: local pharmacist Mike Naglich (a onetime star basketball player himself for Bearcreek, Montana's 1939 small school state champion, which vied for the all-state title that year), who spent the night at the Topper Motel nursing the ailing Locomotives, and Tom Perrigo's mother, Betty, a primary care nurse.

Both veterans played but both were benched in the second half after getting four fouls.

As usual, though, Laurel overcame adversity thanks to teamwork embodied in players stepping up their game when someone else was having a subpar night. Campbell scored 17 points, and Seelye contributed 15 points and 11 rebounds.

Laurel had to rally from a slight first-quarter deficit, 12-10, but the Locomotives led at halftime, 32-23, and after three quarters, 43-34.

Once more, Ready played beyond his years on as big a stage as he could imagine. The sophomore guard hit two free throws with 14 seconds left to ice the game. He added two more free throws at the buzzer, and the Locos had win No. 25.

Both teams shot 47 percent from the field. Laurel's edge came at the free throw line with a 23-of-35 performance compared with Central's 16-for-23 statistics.

The Locomotives' way of defending against sharpshooters throughout the season was to use a diamond-and-one defense, keeping the opposing team's top scoring threat from getting opening looks at the basket. That worked against Sidney's Dave Steinbeisser, and the Locomotives were prepared to use the tactic against Wolf Point's Willie Weeks, a 6-foot-6 senior who many considered the premiere player in the state. Butte Central's upset of the defending champion Wolves in the opening round kept the Locomotives from having to defend Weeks, but it brought a comparable challenge: slowing down Antonietti.

Diamond-and-one, as always, you're one - you've got Antonietti, Tom, Peterson said to Perrigo during pre-game instructions to his club. Perrigo did what was expected, keying on the Maroon star "one" position and helping to hold him to 18 points, almost seven below his season average.

Finally. The championship game against Kalispell, which had defeated Great Falls Russell in the other semifinal, lay ahead for Don Peterson's Locomotives.

CHAPTER 13

The Cinderstellar night

T*hank goodness – it's not so cold tonight,* said a basketball fan in a heavy winter parka, beneath which he wore a shirt decked in purple and gold, Laurel High School's colors.

We've had a heckuva winter, haven't we? he continued, partially unzipping his now too-warm coat.

His companion nodded in agreement.

Doesn't hurt, either, that we've got the hottest team in the state, the second fan said.

As the late-winter sun set behind the snow-capped peaks of the Madison Range to the west, these and other Laurel Locomotives boosters – students, parents and people young and old who just loved high school basketball – streamed toward the doors of the Montana State University Fieldhouse in Bozeman, Montana.

It was about 7 p.m. on March 15, 1969. Spectators wanted to make sure they got inside "The Barn," as the fieldhouse was known then, so they could see the final two games of Montana's state Big 32 tournament. A record 10,700 people attended the Friday night session (more were turned away), so it made sense to find a seat early.

Tip-off for the third-place game, matching Great Falls Russell and Butte Central, was moments away. For many of those strolling toward the arena entrance, however, the real draw was the championship game: Laurel, the state's only unbeaten team with a 25-0 record, versus Flathead of Kalispell, which had a record almost as sparkling (22-3) and a veteran lineup itching to win the trophy after finishing second at state the year before.

While fans waited to get inside, they enjoyed a break from the worst of a cold, snowy winter drawing to an end. The temperature had climbed to 40 degrees that afternoon, a big contrast to Bozeman's 29-below overnight reading earlier in the week.

Any talk of the weather, though, paled compared to excited chatter about the Kalispell-Laurel showdown.

Some Laurel fans asserted that the Locomotives were the best team in the state. Tonight would be their night to prove it by winning the first state basketball championship in school history. No more going to Bozeman for the Big 32 tournament, as Laurel had done the previous three years, just to be competitive but stopped short of claiming the top prize.

Other Laurel fans voiced realism. They repeated what Treasure State sportswriters had noted. Kalispell's imposing front line included a 6-11 junior center who already was drawing interest from major college recruiters. The Braves also started a 6-7 senior forward and had a 6-4 senior reserve. All were capable players who could control the inside game on offense and fend off the Locomotives on defense – no stiffs there.

Meanwhile, Laurel started no one taller than 6-2. In fact, no one on the Locomotives' bench topped 6-2.

The Braves' size advantage correlated with their enrollment edge. Flathead drew its team from a student body of about 1,400, at least triple the enrollment of Laurel – and maybe four times as many students by some accounts that said school enrollment approached 1,700.

This was setting up as a David vs. Goliath scenario. Unlike the Bible, though, David doesn't always win in sports competition.

Wait a minute, the optimists said. *Don't you remember? We've played the big boys before and won. Billings Senior at their place back in December. We beat Bozeman home and away. Great Falls Russell was tough, but we won the divisional championship and handled those guys at their place a couple weeks ago. Don't forget how we crushed Missoula Hellgate right on this floor two nights ago. And remember: last year, right here, we whipped Billings West.*

Plus, the believers reminded the doubters, *we've got one of the best coaches in the state, Don Peterson. He's got a system in place in Laurel where kids learn the Locomotive way starting in the third grade. It's paying off.*

Someone yelled, *Go Locomotives!* They walked through the doors.

Inside the fieldhouse, the largest clear span wooden structure in the world when it opened in 1958, Sally Smith soaked up the atmosphere. She was the lead cheerleader and only senior on Laurel's five-girl cheer squad. She was attending the Big 32 tournament for the fourth time. But this night was different.

Thinking back 45 years to when she had a courtside view of the game, she recalled her emotions:

"It was huge and overwhelming for us – a little Class A town. The crowd was on our side. That was a good feeling."

"Just the excitement of being there," in the big fieldhouse created an unforgettable memory, she said.

"To have the record we had, it was nerve-wracking. Everybody was gunning for you."

As the tip-off drew near, someone else with an insider's knowledge of the matchup sized up the action.

Darrell Ehrlick was a sophomore majoring in accounting at the University of Montana. He had driven from Missoula to Bozeman with friends earlier Saturday to watch the game for two reasons. One, he had been dating Sally Smith for two years, since she was a sophomore and he was a senior at Laurel High School; they later married. Two, as a senior, Ehrlick had been a hot-shooting guard for the Locomotives, setting a school season scoring record of 512 points that still stands. Ehrlick helped lead Laurel into the 1967 State Big 32 tournament, where the Locomotives won their opening game, then lost in the semifinal round and were ousted in Saturday morning, loser-out play.

Would this be the year Laurel won its first state championship? Pondering that question didn't diminish Ehrlick's respect for Kalispell, which many believed deserved the favorite's role because the Braves had the state's dominating player in their lineup that year.

Kalispell's lineup included "Big Brent," 6-11 junior center Brent Wilson, who went on to play Division I basketball at Montana State University and then, as a transfer, at Colorado State University. Wilson, plus a solid supporting cast, gave the Braves the edge on paper, at least, Ehrlick said, recalling his impressions of Laurel's opponent more than four decades after the championship game.

Laurel fans, however, believed the Locomotives could win because of their coach, Don Peterson, an early adopter of the matchup zone defense and a wizard at getting his players to fill roles rather than vying for stardom.

Laurel fans' cautious optimism was countered by many among a sizable Kalispell contingent that had trekked 300 miles from their northwestern Montana city to Bozeman. They hoped to see a different outcome than the year before, when the much-smaller (in enrollment) but talented Wolf Point Wolves beat the Braves for the state championship.

The Braves fans seated on the first level included Rick Weaver, then a junior at Flathead High School and now publisher of the *Daily Interlake* in Kalispell.

"We were screaming for the Braves," he said, thinking back to championship night, although the script he and his friends expected had already been torn up.

"We expected to end up playing Wolf Point for the championship," Weaver said. Butte Central, however, had nixed that prospect, knocking off the Wolves in first-round play.

Whoever ended up being Kalispell's foe in the championship game, Braves fans were confident their team would rule the Big 32.

"I think more than just that (1969 championship) game, if you look at what Flathead High did in my four years there – we had a 93-15 record – we expected to be in the championship game and we expected to win it," Weaver said.

Someone else at the fieldhouse on that never-to-be-forgotten night was Edie Thompson, one of the Locomotives' most loyal fans. She had watched Laurel's home-opener win over Lewistown back in December without her husband. When she came home, she told him he had missing something, that the Locos showed the potential to be a special team. Art Thompson didn't miss a home game the rest of the year.

Asked in March 2016 if she attended the big game, Thompson (whose husband died in 2001) said, "I must have been there because I have programs with all the scores. Time goes by so fast."

She remembered the conventional wisdom before tip-off. "Laurel wasn't expected to win because Kalispell had such tall players."

Mrs. Thompson could claim a link to the MSU Fieldhouse that few others in the crowd could. A native of White Sulphur Springs, she moved a few hundred miles across Montana to Deer Lodge in her youth. There she met and married her husband. Mr. Thompson worked for the Milwaukee Railroad, and his job sent the Thompsons to South Dakota. Still working for the railroad, Thompson was transferred to Three Forks, about 30 miles west of Bozeman. So when the MSU Fieldhouse opened in 1958, the

Thompsons attended the festivities, which allowed attendees to view the completed facility. No special event took place that day at the building, which was designed as an indoor rodeo arena as much as a basketball venue.

"We were at the grand opening, and there was mud about knee-deep out in the parking lot. It was a pretty exciting place. I remember I lost my shoes in the mud," she said.

Smith, Ehrlick, Weaver and Thompson were part of the largest crowd to ever watch a Montana basketball game, at least 10,700 spectators. That surpassed the 10,250 who saw Seattle University and future NBA star Elgin Baylor lead his team to victory over Montana State College (as MSU was known before 1965) in 1958. Spectators got as comfortable as they could on the wooden bleachers, awaiting the tip-off. Though probably no one knew it, they were witnessing the last Big 32 game to be played, and they would see the last Big 32 state championship trophy ever awarded.

As the Locomotives warmed up, trying to keep sky-high emotions in check, they continued trying to adjust to playing in an environment different not only from their own gym but all the typical Montana high school gyms of that era.

"The MSU Fieldhouse was intimidating, and the cavernous darkness all but eliminated any shooter's background," Ric Peterson recalled. "The wall of dark sound was eerie but good, too, because it seemed the Locomotives owned the crowd from the start."

As always, Laurel fans cheered, stomped and joined in as the Locomotives did shootarounds, passed and got ready using their standard choreographed routines.

Peterson said he noticed something interesting overhead, above the scoreboard elevated over the floor: onlookers possibly allowed inside the fieldhouse without tickets due to "inside" connections.

Peterson said he cannot say how many spectators "dangled their feet on high, but it seemed like too many. Suffice to say, there were far more than the advertised number in attendance both Friday and Saturday night. I assume they all climbed safely down – hopefully wearing smiles."

Lane Saunders and Dobbie Lambert, sitting courtside, spoke into microphones mounted on table stands. The two radio broadcasters tuned out the din and shared the charged atmosphere with thousands more fans. Their play-by-play commentary originated at KOOK in Billings, one of Montana's historic stations, and was carried around the Treasure State's vast expanse by affiliated stations.

Some 2,000 miles away, Laurel fan and KBMY announcer Bernie Lustig, spending time in his native New York City, awaited the game broadcast. Someone in Billings, the locality Lustig had chosen to pursue his radio broadcasting career, had made arrangements with Lustig to call him before tip-off and share the game broadcast over the telephone line.

This was long before the Internet made streaming radio broadcasts anywhere in the world an easy, inexpensive experience for anyone with broadband service. Smartphones with audio/video streaming capability? Not even in one's wildest dreams. Instead, Lustig's only listening option involved having someone make a long-distance telephone call to him, with the radio next to the phone receiver. This was when cross-country calls could cost $1 or more per minute. The call came, and he heard the broadcast.

Peterson's pre-game talk in the Laurel locker room set a tone that one of his reserve players, his oldest son Ric, still remembered 45 years later.

"He mentioned things like, 'I'm proud of you guys, you had a great season and it doesn't matter what anybody says – you're champions, no matter what the outcome of the game,' " said the younger Peterson.

Peterson, now living in Dallas where he is an optometrist, remembers the surprised looks his father, who died in 2003, got from that somber send-off.

"We're looking around. He's afraid we might lose. We're not going to lose," Peterson said.

Was it reverse psychology?

"He would never admit one way or the other because I asked him. But sometimes his motivation tactics were a little different," Peterson said, describing his father as anything but a Knute Rockne type of coach. Don Peterson's tactics, though, brought him success equaled by few other high school coaches. He retired with 558 wins (against 238 losses), third-best in state boys basketball history. For reaching the 500-win plateau, he is among a limited number of prep coaches listed at the Naismith Basketball Hall of Fame in Springfield, Massachusetts.

Tip-off was moments away. Don Peterson shared his plan for starting the championship game. The coach's tactic seemed foolhardy to a casual observer: Lee Perrigo, Laurel's 5-8 senior guard, would jump center against Wilson. The Locomotives faced a 15-inch disadvantage in their first ball possession opportunity.

As the Locomotives took the floor for their final warmups, Laurel's pep band struck up another song it had become known for: Al Hirt's "Cotton Candy." It's a piece where trumpeters can shine, and Laurel had a pair of standouts in Dick Cantrell and Tommy Smart, according to Ric Peterson.8

---

8 Peterson said in a 2014 email that Cantrell took piano lessons from his mother, Dorothy, an accomplished musician who still sang in women's groups at church and community functions into her '80s. Cantrell later became a welder in Las Vegas. "Dick used to be a one-man show in taverns and such. I've seen him sit in with house bands in Vegas. He is also beyond amazing on the harmonica and usually carries two or three (in different keys) in his pocket."

Where's Leon ?

Laurel fans settled in their seats and soaked up the big-time atmosphere. Some chatter started. *What's with Leon Schmidt? He played last night against Butte Central. I think he got hurt a bit. Wonder if he can play tonight?*

Schmidt, a 5-10 senior forward, became Laurel's sixth man during the championship season. He scored six points, all on free throws, as the Locomotives held off Butte Central, 63-56, in their Friday night semifinal game. But now he was sitting on the bench in street clothes.

Forty-seven years later, Schmidt detailed what happened. Just before halftime of the semifinal game, with Laurel on its way to a 32-23 lead at intermission, Schmidt sank what he recalled as his 12th or 13th straight free throw – and his high school basketball playing days came to an end.

With a few seconds to go before the break, "I got the ball about midcourt. It ran onto me, and I rolled my ankle hard. To this day, I think I've still got some stain marks in my ankle from the black and blue. After that, I wasn't able to play. I couldn't even walk on that foot."

Schmidt acknowledged that the injury wasn't a fluke. Disregarding Peterson's instructions, he had neglected to tape his ankles, a decision that may have involved his jumping ability. Despite his shortness, Schmidt had enough spring in his legs to leap above the basket. He said he could have dunked the ball if he had had large enough hands to grasp it.

"I can't remember why I didn't tape (the ankles), but it was probably something to do with it might hurt a little bit to jump or land. Maybe I thought I could jump a little higher. It came back and bit me," he said.

On championship Saturday, Schmidt felt blue. "It bothered me a lot," he said, knowing that years of playing basketball in Laurel would end without his getting a chance to contribute to what might become the biggest win of all.

"I took a while to get through it, and my mom really helped me on it," said Schmidt, whose father died when he was 13. He talked to his mother, who he said was a "very religious lady." She said that God may have had a plan for him. "You could have blew that game and look what would have happened. So just sit back and enjoy what you did for the season.

"It was just one of those things when people didn't play because of colds or flu or whatever and miss games. I accepted that," Schmidt said.

Unforgettable start

The Locomotives played for the championship with three ill starters: Bygren (strep throat), and Campbell and Tom Perrigo (both flu-like symptoms). Assistant coach Karl Fiske had a touch of flu, too.

Years later, Lee Perrigo recalled his reaction to Peterson's announcement that he would jump center in place of Bygren. The fellow senior was able to play but was fighting off strep throat he had contracted the day before.

Interviewed in 2014, soon after his retirement after a long career at the Cenex refinery in Laurel, Perrigo said he couldn't remember when coach Peterson told him he would jump center.

A memorable picture (reportedly taken by photographer Jim Scott, for the *Laurel Leaves* school newspaper and part of the book cover) depicts the center-jump mismatch better than words. The photo, which probably was taken by Laurel High student newspaper photographer Jim Scott, shows Wilson at the peak of his leap, his arms stretched to maximum length. Perrigo, though, elevates to less than the 15 inches he gave up to his rival, likely due to better jumping ability.

Ric Peterson, who later coached military service teams and says he often conferred with his father about coaching tactics, said, "Coach set up an offensive play and looking at that picture, Wilson had just tipped it so the ball is almost straight above us."

"There's three Kalispell guys on the circle and only one Laurel guy. Tom Perrigo is on the circle. So the other three (Locomotives) were working the play, which meant we were going to guess where we thought he was going to tip it to."

The other three Laurel players stayed off the circle, allowing them to move as soon as the ball was whistled in play.

"As soon as the ball was tipped, Bygren, Seelye and Campbell made their cuts to try to intercept the pass, where we thought he'd tip it to," Lee Perrigo said.

The Locos coaching staff had scouted the Braves and noticed Wilson's tendency to tip the ball behind him, where a teammate could grab it.

Peterson devised a play to give one of his three players positioned off the circle a chance to intercept a backward tip. Then, the tactic was to have other two players break for the basket, setting up a potential 3-on-1 scoring break.

"So that was the idea. It wasn't just a gimmick to play with their head," Lee Perrigo said.

"You can imagine if we were to get the opening tip and score on it, that's going to be huge. That's going to get the momentum swung immediately," he said.

Going small to start the game worked well in the view of Laurel players. If nothing else, it made for a never-to-be-forgotten experience for Perrigo – and an amazing sight for the record crowd packed inside the fieldhouse.

The KOOK broadcasters described the sights and sounds to listeners around the state, plus some of an estimated 500 people who were turned away at the gate and returned to the parking lot to listen to the game on their car radios.

"Kalispell's one nice team," Saunders told listeners. "They've got the height, the nice guards. It's going to be quite a ball game here."

Lambert, former coach of the Montana State College Bobcats basketball team[9], told the radio audience that Laurel would count on its outside shooting, speed and ball-handling savvy to offset Kalispell's "overpowering height."

Expanding on Saunders' estimate that one-fourth of spectators, more than 2,500, were "solid Laurel fans," Lambert said, "They've worked up into a frenzy, and the emotions are flowing. Adrenaline is getting high, and we're going to have some kind of a contest."

The Braves came out playing a 2-3 zone defense, keeping Wilson, 6-7 Don Groven and 6-4 Greg Ellingson underneath the basket to grab rebounds. If Kalispell stayed in that set, which had helped it win its first two state tournament games, the much smaller Locomotives would have trouble getting second shots, Lambert predicted.

Peterson's ploy, sending Perrigo against Wilson for the game-opening center jump, worked. The Braves controlled the ball and fed it to Gary Stoick. He missed a long jumper, and the Locos' Bygren rebounded. Kalispell regained possession, but Campbell stole the ball and passed to Seelye. The senior forward sank a jump shot, Laurel took the initial lead, and the Laurel-leaning throng exulted.

---

9 Lambert coached the Bobcats in two 1958 games against Elgin Baylor-led Seattle University. (Baylor went on to National Basketball Association stardom.) Playing at home, the Chieftans won the first contest on January 15, 1958, 108-83, as Baylor scored a then-school record 53 points. Afterwards, Lambert said, "Baylor's fantastic. He certainly has a variety of shots. Some I've never seen before." The Chieftans came to Bozeman for a February 20, 1958, game. This time, Montana State led, 77-74, with 45 seconds to play and stood a chance of upsetting the 17thranked visitors. The Chieftans, however, used a long set shot by Jim Haynes to pull out a 78-77 win. The Bobcats got the satisfaction of having held Baylor, the nation's scoring leader with a 34.4 points per game average, to 23 points. The rematch attracted 10,250 spectators - a record attendance for any Montana basketball game that stood until at least 10,700 people attended each of the final two sessions of the 1969 State Big 32 tournament, the Friday night semifinals and the Saturday night consolation and championship games.

CHAPTER 14

Win the last of 'em all

"I've been working on the railroad," blared the Laurel pep band, its music welcome but hardly needed to keep the raucous Locomotive fans at high intensity as the contested game neared its finish.

Seven lead changes occurred in the first quarter before Kalispell edged ahead, 10-9, as Jim Otten got a bunny with just under two minutes left. The Braves' Groven used his five-inch advantage over the Locomotives' front-liners to tap in an offensive rebound, and Gary Hall and Wilson added free throws to put Kalispell up, 14-11.

Laurel's ace, Campbell, connected from the top of the key to trim Kalispell's lead to one, 14-13. The Locomotives also got a lift from deadly shooting by Seelye, who took advantage of the Braves' 2-1-2 zone and got open shots. He hit all three of his tries from the field midway through the first quarter.

The packed house saw something that many in the crowd reminisce about more than four decades later.

With time running out, Hall took a pass at midcourt. The Braves guard barely stopped before his 40-foot heave, a swisher at the buzzer that brought the Kalispell fans to their feet and put the Braves up by three, 16-13.

Still, the first quarter portended what laid ahead.

Laurel usually deployed Don Peterson's trademark "modulated, stratified defense," which was a part zone, part man-to-man defense, with guards playing zone and the front line playing man. Against Kalispell, however, Peterson used what he called a "Chinese" defense, a variation on a triangle-and-2 defense, to contain Wilson. Lee Perrigo positioned himself behind Wilson, moving him off the blocks and beyond his range, while Bygren fronted Wilson to deny him the "invite" pass.

Here's how it looked to Lambert, as he spoke into a KOOK microphone.

"Laurel has decided to turn (Kalispell's) Jim Otten loose and double-team the big man," Lambert told listeners.

"They're going to give Otten the outside shot until he proves he can make it. He's had three shots already and hasn't made any of them. It remains to be seen whether the boy can because they're double-teaming Wilson."

Laurel counted on Otten's tendency to allow his elbow to fly while shooting, reducing his accuracy. It was a calculated risk that paid off.

The Braves grabbed a 28-20 lead with about 2½ minutes left in the first half, getting a three-point play from Groven, who was fouled on a successful follow-up shot and then added the free throw. The Locomotives, however, answered with Bygren's basket in the key and four consecutive points by Tom Perrigo. He canned a long jumper, then made both ends of a one-and-one free throw opportunity. That made it Kalispell 28, Laurel 26 at halftime.

Some Laurel boosters, co-workers in the town's Northern Pacific Railroad yards, could have exchanged knowing glances at that point. *Sure feels like a long, hard day at the roundhouse,* someone might have said.

Kalispell grabbed leads of four points (30-26) and five points (32-27) early in the third quarter, on Otten and Wilson baskets, respectively, but two stalwarts brought the Locomotives back.

Seelye connected from the corner to make it 32-29, and Campbell drained a 15-footer and a 10-footer to give the guys in purple a 33-32 advantage.

After Kalispell's Groven converted a free throw to make it 35-all, the Locomotives took control. Two Tom Perrigo free throws put the Locos up, 37-35. Wilson was called for a charge, his fourth foul, and Ready's free throw put Laurel up, 38-35, with 2:41 left in the frame.

Tom Perrigo converted a bonus, giving Laurel five unanswered points and a 40-35 lead. Hall broke the run with a free throw, but Bygren scored on a put-back and drew Groven's fourth foul.

The quarter neared its end. Kalispell coach Paul Gologoski had benched Wilson but he sent the big junior back in. The Braves' center was drawing as many as four defenders, leaving teammate Otten loose on the wing.

Wilson sank a free throw, trimming the Braves' deficit to 43-37 with 1:40 left, but Laurel answered. Lee Perrigo canned an uncontested shot for a 45-37 lead – Laurel's largest of the game – as the third quarter ended. Yet, that margin seemed shaky given the game tempo.

Can Laurel prevail?

As the fourth quarter began, the Braves made another run. An Otten bucket and two Groven tip-ins pulled Kalispell within two, 45-43. Basket-trading ensued, Tom Perrigo and Seelye connecting for Laurel, Stoick and Groven (on an assist from Wilson) responding for Kalispell. That left the Locos up by 49-47 – and brought the crowd to its feet, cheering at a frenzied pitch.

Again, Campbell sparkled. He got open in the corner and swished a 20-footer. Laurel led, 51-47, at 5:43 in the fourth quarter. Kalispell responded: reliable senior Stoick hit both shots of a one-and-one to make it 51-49.

Tom Perrigo got a steal and the Locos attacked the Braves' 2-3 zone. Kalispell got the ball back, and Groven's 6-7 height allowed him to sink a close-range shot. 51-all. 3:25 left.

Once more, the Locomotives rolled ahead, Campbell drawing a foul and converting a bonus situation to make it 53-51. The final 2:50 sent the huge, raucous crowd into still-higher decibel range. Looking up from his seat inside the massive building, a fan said, *Do you think we might blow the roof off?*

Stoick's fourth foul sent Campbell to the line again. He missed the front of a one-and-one, and Kalispell rebounded. The Braves couldn't capitalize, giving up the ball when Groven was called for charging defender Tom Perrigo. It was Groven's fifth foul. There went one-third of the Braves' overwhelming frontline advantage.

Perrigo, facing a one-and-one with a chance to pad Laurel's tenuous lead if not salt away the win, missed the first shot. The Braves again gained possession, broke Laurel's press and worked the ball inside to Wilson. *Defense! Stop the big guy*! Laurel fans hollered. To no avail. The junior center's layup made it 53-all. 1:50 left.

After Bygren missed a short shot, Laurel continued to press the Braves as they tried to set up the last shot. That effort failed because Otten, their senior guard, committed an offensive foul. Then it was Laurel's turn to lose an opportunity, as smooth playmaker Campbell traveled.

That set up a minute of drama that no one who played in, or watched, the game will ever forget.

Otten shot and missed an open jumper from the left side. He got another open look and put up another jumper. Miss! Ellingson rebounded, and Braves' coach Paul Gologoski called time out with 1:03 remaining to set up the potential winning play; he told the squad to use a play they had practiced many times and used in previous games.

The Braves inbounded to Stoick who passed to Otten, who passed to Wilson. The big center, a lefthander, rolled off a high screen and broke down the left side. About 20 seconds remained when Ellingson broke free on the right side, underneath the basket. Wilson saw him and whistled a pass to the senior forward.

Laurel fans groaned in disbelief. Their magic season and magic night seemed to slipping away at that instant.

Then the unbelievable happened. The ball hit Ellingson's knee and caromed out of bounds. Gologoski, the veteran coach who guided Kalispell into the 1968 and 1969 state Big 32 championship games, provided the most detailed description of the play that relegated his Braves to a bridesmaid role for the second year in a row.

Gologoski, a native of the Montana Hi-Line town of Havre, had taken over the helm in Kalispell in 1966. He thus got a chance to develop most of the players on his senior-loaded 1969 squad, plus junior big man Wilson.

"The thing that stands out was we lost it right at the end," Gologoski said in 2014, the year he turned 84. He lived in an assisted-living facility in Kalispell, his mind sharp as he conversed over the phone despite suffering a stroke a decade earlier.

"We got the ball out of bounds underneath our basket. I had a reserve in there. Of course, Wilson was my big gun.

"Everybody thought we were going to go to Wilson," and, sensing that, Gologoski told his team to use another proven play. "So, (for) the out-of-bounds play we had set up – and it was not something we had thought up spur of the moment; we'd run it all year long – we would break a kid open and he would screen for Wilson and roll to the basket."

The usual sequence then was for the cutter to pass back to Wilson, who was positioned for an easy basket.

"We did this in the championship game and did it perfectly, except when we passed the ball inbounds to my ballplayer who was rolling underneath (Ellingson), he just fumbled the ball. He hit it with his knee and knocked it of bounds.

"That one little simple play, and we would have won the game instead of losing it," Gologoski said.

"I've often wondered why I didn't just pass it to Wilson. I thought everybody would be moving towards him. That's the way it turned out – the kid just accidentally ... the pass was a little low and as he reached for it, he bumped it with his knee instead of getting it in his hands and it rolled out of bounds again. That was it."

The muffed pass gave the Locomotives another chance to win, possibly their last in regulation play, with 17 seconds left. They set up a shot against a Kalispell defense that was still stout despite the loss of Groven.

Laurel's possession caused its fans to have another hold-your-breath moment. The Locomotives ran the clock down to two seconds when Tom Perrigo drew Wilson's fifth foul. He headed the bench, a spectator for whatever would happen next.

Perrigo walked to the line, paused for a moment and fired his first shot of a one-and-one, with the chance to win the game and be the hero. He missed. The buzzer sounded. Regulation play had ended. *We'll play overtime, guys,* one ref said.

Those final seconds just before overtime are etched in Perrigo's memory, almost 50 years later.

"When I missed the free throw, I was devastated. Thank goodness we won as I would have been a goat for life," he said in 2014.

Bygren was one of Perrigo's best friends in high school, and they've remained close in adulthood despite being half a world apart. The onetime Laurel center also remains good friends with a teammate who's closer, current Texas resident Campbell, who is the other member of the Locomotive twosome who could have won the championship game in regulation but missed a clutch free-throw attempt near the end.

Bygren said Perrigo's "never heard the end of that," his whiff of the last-second free throw. Expanding his good-natured ribbing to include Campbell, Bygren said other teammates "always told them how lucky they were to have Lee and I on the team. Otherwise, they might not have won the state championship." Not only did Bygren and Lee Perrigo check Brent Wilson, Metzger contributed several forearm checks on the Braves' center. Wilson blocked several shots, but the swarming Locos forced him to alter several shots. This drained his energy and reduced his effectiveness, which was a vital contribution to the Laurel win.

Overtime

Kalispell's two big men, Wilson and Groven, nine inches and five inches, respectively, taller than the tallest Locomotives, watched from the bench as the Locomotives took charge in overtime. Bygren, who anchored the Locos' front line despite the strep throat that weakened him the night before, sank two free throws to put the Trainmen ahead for good, 55-53. Ellingson answered for Kalispell, sinking a free throw to make it 55-54.

Lee Perrigo, who was in the spotlight when the game began, punctuated the championship. The 5-8 senior dribbled, helping the Locomotives work their Dean Smith four-corner offense in the final minute. He saw a lane to the hoop, swooped in for a layup, and the scoreboard read: Laurel 57, Kalispell 54. Game over.

Perrigo earned a place in Montana prep basketball history because his were the last points scored in a Big 32 game.

Saunders, one of the KOOK broadcasters, captured the moment then – and for posterity, thanks to a recording made of the broadcast. "Pandemonium breaks loose at the fieldhouse. The Laurel Locomotives are the new 1968-69 Big 32 champions. And there's a happy, happy crew on the floor right now. Looks like a pack of ants. Only undefeated team in the state of Montana," he said over the air.

Gologoski said the intervening decades have softened his view of the game, putting it in a positive light, if not making it glow.

"That was a good ball game, and Laurel was a great ball club. They deserved to win. I didn't think so at the time, but they were a championship team," he said.

CHAPTER 15

Let's look at the Film

Don Peterson was ahead of his time as a high school basketball coach in the 1960s, according to players on teams that competed against Laurel. His former players agree, as do fellow faculty members at the high school and several opposing coaches.

A good example of Peterson's innovation involved filming games of future Locomotive foes. This was when scouting for most high school basketball coaches meant placing a phone call to a coaching friend who already had played the team in question and asking him to describe the its strengths and weaknesses. With luck, the coaching friend might even detail the style of individual players.

Filming opponents was then largely limited to the college ranks. Peterson, though, emulated his peers higher on the coaching ladder. To get footage of opponents he could study before upcoming games, he enlisted the help of a teacher who had just come to Laurel and who learned how to film basketball games on the fly.

That scout-in-the-making was Dick Hatfield, hired as a junior high school counselor in 1968. Hatfield had been teaching in Cody, Wyoming, and was working toward his master's degree in counseling.

Approaching his 84th birthday when interviewed in early 2016, Hatfield said the Cody system treated him well.

"They've got a good salary system down there – a lot better than Montana's. I always joked with Peterson that, 'Hey, your getting me up here cost me about 10 grand,' " said Hatfield, who continued living in Laurel after his retirement.

Besides counseling, Hatfield knew sports, particularly baseball and basketball. A native of north-central Pennsylvania, he was signed by the Detroit Tigers in the early 1950s. He pitched a couple of seasons in the Tigers farm system and made the big club roster for spring training in 1958.

Before that, he started college at a small school in Ohio.

"I played basketball with one of the great, all-time college teams, they say." That was the 1953 squad at Rio Grande College in Ohio. The star of the team, Bevo Francis, scored 113 points against Hillsdale College in 1954, a single-game individual scoring record that stood until 2012. He later signed with Boston Whirlwinds, a barnstorming team that played against the Harlem Globetrotters. Francis died in 2015.

It was during the Cold War. Hatfield was drafted and joined the Air Force. He was discharged but still in the reserves, so the military could call someone like him up for a 30-day deployment.

"I got recalled back in the military. That's how I got to Montana," Hatfield said.

He got to choose where he wanted to go. He requested Malmstrom Air Force Base in Great Falls, and the Air Force obliged. He ended up at a radar site near the Canadian border. The closest town, ironically, was Cut Bank, where Don Peterson had grown up.

"I decided to get out of the military and go back to college. I finished at Rocky Mountain College (in Billings). I couldn't play, although I was offered a scholarship. I was 31 years old," he said.[10]

Soon after getting to Laurel, Hatfield was asked if he'd hit the road to film opponents and scout them.

"I didn't know much about cameras – press the button and it turns on; press it and it turns off. A lot of times, I turned it off when I should've turned it on," Hatfield said.

Hatfield had gotten to know Tom Wilson, one of Peterson's assistant coaches when Hatfield and Wilson were both teaching in Belfry and were neighbors there. Still, Hatfield had to define what Peterson could expect from him.

"Their idea was to have me primarily as a scout associated with the basketball team. And I had to prompt him, 'Hey, my counseling comes first.' "

The Laurel school superintendent respected the boundaries between counseling and scouting, how Hatfield couldn't sacrifice time in the office so he could make long road trips to attend games of future Locomotive opponents. The coaches, however, didn't understand Hatfield's firm stand at first but eventually assented.

---

[10] One of Hatfield's classmates at Rocky, "my old buddy," as he put it, was Tom Ferch. The Circle, Montana, native later became coach at Park County High School in Livingston. The Ferch-coached Rangers won state Class A championships in 1983 and 1985 behind the spectacular play of his sons, Kral and Shann. Montana State recruited Kral Ferch, and he led the Bobcats on a storybook run to the Big Sky conference championship in 1986. He scored 54 points in the final two Big Sky tournament games to lead the Bobcats to upset wins over Northern Arizona and the University of Montana. Kral Ferch, who was named to the Bobcat Hall of Fame in 2011, was known for his dunking ability. *Sports Illustrated* magazine called him "an eyeful." Montana college basketball fans still talk about his dunk against St. John's in the NCAA tournament. Younger brother Shann played with Kral for two years at MSU before transferring to Pepperdine.

"I never expected or collected a cent of travel allowance from the school to do that. It was against my grain to do that," Hatfield said.

He did, however, set a non monetary price for his scouting services, something based on patriotism and his military service, and while the Vietnam War was raging and respect for the flag was at low ebb. "It was terrible there for a while," he said, so Hatfield gave the Laurel players a mandate. "I said on the day you guys don't stand at attention with your hand over your heart at the pre-game national anthem, I'm resigning."

That never happened. He continued scouting.

When Hatfield returned from a trip, he'd give the camera, film still inside, to Peterson for express processing at a film developer in Billings. "Oftentimes, he would invite me in (to midweek sessions with the team) to give any added commentary for what it was worth."

Hatfield remembers the time, in the late 1960s and early 1970s, as a period when Montana was blessed with "a lot of good players – every team had 'em."

When Hatfield got to a gym, he always bought two programs, using one as a worksheet on which he jotted notes. Those notes were as useful as the film, he said, and a program provided the only means of identifying players – by their numbers – because uniforms didn't have player names on them.

Hatfield said he missed attending the 1969 Big 32 state championship game.

"They (Kalispell) had that big seven-footer," actually 6-11 junior center Brent Wilson. "I scouted him. I don't know where it was – Billings, Bozeman? He had some weaknesses, and Pete took advantage of it. He didn't have a good championship game. They held them down."

Hatfield shared memories of Peterson's coaching, prefacing them by saying he remains amazed that the 1969 team, with no one taller than 6-2, was always the smallest team on the floor. Yet the Locomotives beat the odds and ran the table that year.

"The thing that amazed me about Don Peterson is his plays were so complex. I wondered how in the world players ever understood to carry 'em out. Actually, looking at them they didn't. They went out and kind of played their own game. That was my opinion.

Ric Peterson confirmed Hatfield's observation. He said Campbell and Lee Perrigo, who both were in their first year in the Laurel system, sometimes got lost in the Laurel's complicated defensive schemes. Other players also got out of synch sometimes, "but there just enough conformance to win it all," Peterson said.

Hatfield said, "The other thing about Don Peterson is with two minutes left on the clock and a close game, I don't think there's any better coach in the nation than Don Peterson. He had a way to win."

Peterson's focus on defense was the key to his becoming one of Montana's best prep coaches. "That's what wins championships," Hatfield said.

Hatfield and Peterson bonded outside sports, too, through a shared interest in art.

"Don was an avid art collector," according to Hatfield. "I probably spent more time scouting artwork for him than anything. Here's a guy (who) can win championships. He's cool, calm and collected. Hardly forces a smile. Of course, he gave credit to his players, which I appreciated. But to see him get emotional over a painting – that was something."

CHAPTER 16

Kalispell Braves: Laurel won but …

Bitterness about the outcome of the state championship game lingers to this day among Braves backers, more than 47 years after the Laurel-Kalispell showdown as of the publication of this book. Dissatisfaction is pronounced among Kalispell residents who cheered for the 1969 Braves as high school students, some of whom who may have made the 300-mile trip to Bozeman to watch the tournament, according to former Braves player Don Groven.

Groven said the Locomotives' techniques for drawing fouls removes some of the afterglow from their victory.

He called the Locomotives "chintzy" for running down the court and then falling to draw fouls when they fronted the Braves.

Recalling the first half of the game, Groven said, "Laurel would run down the court and get in front of Brent (Wilson)" so that an offensive foul would be charged to the Braves' 6-11 junior center. "They did that twice. The third time, the referees called it on Laurel.

That kind of stuff – it's a tough way to win, and a lot of people remember that."

From a Laurel standpoint, the tactic of stationing Lee Perrigo in front of Wilson, hoping for a charge, made sense. Perrigo forced the taller and heavier Wilson to change direction several times, and inevitable fatigue caused his play to slump.

Thinking back, Ric Peterson said this was not a rule violation, despite what Braves fans might maintain. He remembers Perrigo drawing two charges from Wilson, "and maybe Lee wasn't set the third time, but Wilson had a long run from end to end all night."

Don Peterson's coaching brilliance stands out in the mind of the Laurel player on whom the strategy of negating Kalispell's height advantage focused: Lee Perrigo.

Perrigo said his coach was thinking about a possible Laurel-Kalispell match even before the state tournament and gave him the game plan in practice.

"He had me guarding Brent Wilson. If we play Kalispell, this is what I want you to do: take as many charges as you can. We have to get him out of the game," Perrigo said in 2014.

Because the Locomotives had no one whose height approached Wilson's, they devised a workaround that the stand-in for the Kalispell center used. Junior varsity player Gary Whitney, who stood 6-2, was a stand-in for Wilson in practice; Whitney held a broom over his head as he moved against Perrigo.

Perrigo described his coach's instructions:

"Every time (Wilson) went down court, (Peterson) wanted me to run backwards in front of him. And if he turned his head, I was supposed to plant and let him run over me. All of a sudden, there it was – he didn't even mention it to me (in the championship game). I started doing it when I had a chance. I started planting when he was in front of me."

Perrigo said Wilson ran over him three times. The first time, "I thought it was a solid charge but they called the foul on me." From then on, though, Wilson's moves in Perrigo's direction resulted in offensive fouls.

"He felt like I was a little gnat buzzing around his head, and then he popped me good. Under the basket, he swung his arm around and knocked me about 20 feet. He got a foul out of that. So the plan of getting him out of the game eventually worked because late in the game, he fouled out," Perrigo said.

One play stands out in Groven's mind. With about two minutes left in regulation and Laurel leading, 53-51, Groven made a jump shot that would have tied the score. Instead, he was called for an offensive foul, sending Tom Perrigo to the line. Perrigo missed the front end, Kalispell rebounded, and the Braves tied it at 53 on Wilson's layup at the 1:50 mark. No more scoring occurred in the fourth quarter, sending the contest into overtime.

Recalling his thwarted basket, which might have helped Kalispell win the game, Groven said, "I don't remember touching anybody." It was Groven's fifth foul. "I've heard a lot of people say that was (Laurel's) big thing," having Groven foul out.

"I still don't understand how I got called for it. It was a fade-away jump shot. I don't know who I touched. I never felt anything."

Groven believes Laurel wanted him and Wilson out of the game because the two big men controlled play in the second half. Fouling out "two of the best players in the state" gave the smaller Locomotives the winning edge, he asserted.

Groven, now retired from his job as a tire store manager in Havre, said he stays in contact with former teammates and others who rooted for the Braves.

"I heard a lot from Kalispell," especially after the *Billings Gazette* and the *Kalispell Daily Interlake* published 45th anniversary stories about the epic game in March and April 2014. "Their perspective remains that Laurel beat us, but they didn't beat us with our best players on the floor."

Wilson and Groven both picked up their fifth fouls late in the fourth quarter, and Ellingson fouled out in overtime. No one from Laurel fouled out. Kalispell picked up 26 fouls, Laurel 16. However, the Locomotives, normally excellent free-throw shooters, didn't capitalize on their advantage. They converted just 15 of 29 attempts.

"Groven said it is a tough way to win – I agree, yes it is," Peterson said.

"The Trainmen had to derail the Braves somehow, and the size mismatch was all but overwhelming. The Locos, however, were better-conditioned athletes, especially Lee who was very strong and pushed on Wilson, sapping energy throughout the contest," he said.

When Perrigo needed a breather, Coach Peterson didn't lack for a capable replacement: all-state football linebacker Metzger went in.

"It is withering just thinking of what Wilson absorbed in that contest," Ric Peterson said, adding that the Locomotives' pre-game warmup routine also may have won over some fans and helped Laurel gain the crowd advantage.

Wilson, interviewed by phone from his home in Phoenix in 2014, had just finished listening to a recording of the 1969 state championship game broadcast. That refreshed his memory and allowed him to get in a dig at the officiating.

"The announcer (KOOK's Lane Saunders) said 'He's (Wilson) going to have to play like he's on eggshells now' " after picking up his third foul midway through the second quarter. Relying on Saunders' description, Wilson said, "One of your (Laurel) guys shot a 30-footer. They called a foul on me for (contact with) a guy who shot a 30-footer? I must have turned around too fast. I mean there wasn't even a rebound. How could I have fouled someone?" Wilson asked, disbelief in his voice.

After leading Kalispell to the State AA championship in 1970, the year after the Big 32 dissolved, during a contest in which he scored a state championship game record 51 points against Helena, Wilson signed with Montana State University. He started one year for the Bobcats, then transferred to what he called the "graveyard" of college basketball at the time, Colorado State University, where he earned his degree. He met Phil Jackson when the former New York Knicks star and later NBA coaching great moved to Montana's Flathead area in 1974. That meeting resulted in a NBA tryout for Wilson, in which he guarded Lonnie Shelton, who played on the Seattle Supersonics' 1979 championship team.

Well before college basketball and his outside shot at playing professionally, Wilson said he had learned not to be fazed by a big-game atmosphere such as the Laurel-Kalispell game.

"I was never affected by a crowd," he said. He noticed how big the crowd was that night at the MSU Fieldhouse – almost 11,000 people, a state record for any basketball game. "It was packed," he said, adding that his parents drove to the tournament from Kalispell and he had trouble helping them find seats in the fieldhouse.

Wilson said he knew the teams would play in front of a "monstrous (crowd) because everybody from Laurel was probably there and half of Billings," which was then becoming Montana's biggest city.

"The more antagonistic the crowd, the more I loved it. I was one of those players who usually played better away than at home," he said, explaining that hostile fans energized him.

"I didn't mind, but the referees listened to it also. Of all the games I've played in, I felt that game was seven against five because of the referees," Wilson said.

Just like Groven, the fifth foul that Wilson picked up is engraved in his mind and remains an annoyance.

"I was going for ball. It wasn't even a rebound," Wilson said. He remembers taking "a swipe at a guy." However, "I didn't even cause wind to go by." The whistle blew. "The referee may as well have called it in from Billings." Wilson's night and season were over.

Earlier, after getting his third foul in the second quarter, Wilson was benched. Kalispell held a two-point halftime lead and was up by three points early in the third quarter when he came back in. He was gone, though, when the Braves could have used him most.

"I think if me and Brent would have been able to stay in the game, it would have been a different game," Groven said. Yet, he added, "that's how it ends. It's part of the game."

Groven expressed admiration for Laurel coach Don Peterson and what he got from his undersized roster. "Laurel was an excellent team. They had some good ball players," he said.

Peterson's successful tactic was to put a defender in front of one of the Braves' frontline players and one behind him. Then, when the Braves missed an outside shot, Laurel was in a better rebounding position thanks to overloading the zone, Groven said.

"We should have went to man-to-man, but our coach just sat there on a lump," he said.

Groven said Peterson "virtually won the game."

"The teams were equal," he said, "and I think in some ways we had an advantage because of our size. What was different was Peterson willed them to win. He did what he had to make them win."

CHAPTER 17

Kudos from fellow coaches and arch-rivals

"Congratulations on the terrific season. I really enjoyed watching your club in action. For my money, it was the finest disciplined ball club I have ever watched."

That's how a March 27, 1969, letter from Bill Racicot to Don Peterson began. Racicot was coach of the men's basketball team at Carroll College. He had come to the Helena, Montana, school from the northwestern Montana town of Libby. There, he coached the Loggers, another Class A team moved into the Big 32, to the 1966 state championship – the first of three Big 32 titles won by smaller Class A schools competing against bigger Class AA opponents. The Loggers' championship roster included Racicot's son, Marc, a future attorney general and governor of Montana.

Bill Racicot closed his letter by lauding Peterson for a "wonderful season. It couldn't (have) happened to a finer coach. I must repeat again – it was terrific!"

Peterson and the Locomotives got a special letter a few days after winning the championship; it came from a coach of a rival Big 32 school who also had ties to the railroad town. Laurel native Dan Freund, coach of Glasgow, extended congratulations and continued:

"Naturally I would have rather it had been my own Scotties in that game, but since we weren't and since I'm an 'old' Locomotive, I pulled for you all the way.

"What the Locomotives lacked in size and talent, they made up for in every other department. But I think the most impressive thing, at least to me, was the tremendous team play and unselfishness of the ball club, not only the players on the floor, but your bench as well. The boys who didn't play much should have won the cheerleading award. They had great spirit."

Freund said the championship team was a credit to their town and to basketball. Peterson, he said, enhanced the coaching profession, not only because of his technical ability to teach all aspects of the sport but because he instilled "great desire, spirit and team play as well."

Refuting disparagement of the Locomotives and their fans by the *Great Falls Tribu*ne that season, Freund said, "I would have awarded the Sportsmanship Trophy to Laurel."

Accolades also came from a perhaps unlikely source. The student body at Billings Central High School, Laurel's arch-rivals, wrote to the Locomotives after the 1969 state tournament.

"Twenty-six and 0 and no more to go stands very well by itself," the letter said, adding that Laurel's players and coaches should be proud "for pushing to a tremendous season; one that will be remembered for a long time."

CHAPTER 18

Big 32 a big, brief hit

Laurel, the final state Big 32 champion in 1969, and Wolf Point, which ruled the league a year earlier, had able company in the elite ranks those years: the Flathead Braves of Kalispell.

During a four-year span, 1967-1970, the Gologoski-coached Braves compiled a 93-15 record. They twice were state runners-up, to Wolf Point and Laurel. The Braves got a championship in 1970 (after the Big 32 was disbanded), when Wilson scored a state-record 51 points against Helena in the AA final. That team also featured an outstanding defender, Sam McCullum, better known for his football play at Montana State University and in the NFL for the Seattle Seahawks and the Minnesota Vikings.

Groven, a senior forward on Kalispell's 1969 team, earned a scholarship to Northern Montana College in Havre, where he played for the Northern Lights and still holds the school career rebounding record. Groven said the Big 32 may have been the best thing to happen in Montana prep basketball history. The sense of heightened competition was exciting and drew fans in numbers unmatched today, when Montana's population has nearly doubled.

"The whole thing that year was ... wild," Groven said in a 2014 interview.

"When we played the divisional championship against Columbia Falls, they were scalping tickets for a high school game – believe it or not – for $500, $600. A guy offered, I think it was $200, for my mom's tickets. She turned it down. It was quite a deal."

Flathead's gym seated about 4,500 according to Groven.

"It was wall to wall. There was a real craze back then – I think more than now.

"But there wasn't all the TV stuff," he said, referring to a constant menu of college and professional basketball games available to channel surfers today. "That made a difference."

Kalispell coach Gologoski assembled a standout group of assistant coaches, which included Bill Epperly. Epperly later became head coach at Lewistown, where his Golden Eagles played Don Peterson's Locomotives in the 1970s. Epperly returned to the Flathead in the early 1980s and coached the Braves for several years.

Now retired and living in Kalispell, Epperly, in a 2014 interview, echoed Groven's comments about community backing for the Braves in the late 1960s and early 1970s.

"There were some great crowds in those days. The next year when we beat Helena for the title, it was the same. There was 10,000-plus for the championship game" at the MSU Fieldhouse.

"It was something else in those days. One of the reasons I think (was) the Big 32 really created the interest because the medium and small schools were going against one another. It was a great time for crowds and for basketball interest."

Overflow crowds at the Laurel-Kalispell game, and the semifinal games the night before, pushed the overall 1969 tournament attendance to 41,000. Even allowing for double-counting of people who attended multiple sessions, that amounted to a sizable percentage of Montana's total population, which was 694,000 in the 1970 census. Despite the obvious crowd appeal, representatives of the Montana High School Association's Class AA and A schools, those making up the Big 32, voted, 19-13, to disband the six-year-old league at a special meeting in April 1969.

Groven expressed his regret at the passing of the Big 32 in strong terms.

"To be honest with you, I think they (the Montana High School Association) screwed up by (disbanding the Big 32). I think it was (a matter) of the big schools not wanting to get beat by the little schools," he said.

Groven noted that when Kalispell won the Class AA/Big 16 title in 1970, the Braves' only loss was to a Little 16/Class A school, Whitefish. Whitefish capped that season by beating Laurel for the state Big 16 championship.

Dave Brinkel, a reserve on the championship team, agrees with Groven in thinking big-school disgruntlement caused the Big 32 to be scuttled

"I will always believe the Big 32 was taken away because there were too many small schools beating the big boys," he said. The smaller school included Libby, Wolf Point and Laurel, all championship winners; and Columbia Falls, a second-place finisher. Thus, Class A boasted a title winner or runner up four of the six years that the Big 32 existed, which, in Brinkel's view, prompted AA administrators to use "some political clout" to sway the MHSA to drop the league in the spring of 1969.

"And I have always thought that Laurel winning the Big 32 that year was the last straw they would accept. They didn't want any more small schools competing against them. They wanted to have their own event ... and they're the ones who are the king of the castle," he said.

Norm Clarke, a dean of Montana sportswriters who reported the 1969 tournament for the *Billings Gazette*, pulled no punches when describing why the league folded.

In a Facebook message from Las Vegas, where he is the *Review-Journal's* man-about-town columnist, Clarke said the "big-school vote to go back to (the) previous alignment after the embarrassment of losing to the Class A schools was shameful. They had a magical formula with the Big 32 and blew it."

Why? "Because they wanted to cover their (backsides)," he said.

Groven often hears from someone close to him who agrees that the glory days of Montana high school basketball were during the Big 32 era. "My sister says every time she watches the Hoosiers (movie), it's the same basic thing," he said.

CHAPTER 19

A star says no to college basketball

Ask Montana basketball people who was the best player on Laurel's championship team, and you'll likely get two answers: Campbell and Tom Perrigo. Both were all-state selections during the Locomotives' 26-0 season.

Spoon, a former teammate of both, is an unquestioned backer of Perrigo as the best of a squad that epitomized team play without star power. Spoon's declaration of Perrigo's heads-above-the-rest talent gets backing from someone who played with him at the next level, on Montana State University's freshman basketball team of 1969-70, former Bozeman Holy Rosary star Scott Koelzer.

Spoon, reflecting in 2016 on what happened more than four decades earlier, noted that coach Don Peterson brought Perrigo up to the Locomotives varsity as a sophomore. Not that Peterson was on a desperate search for underclass help to bolster a subpar team – he already had Bob Crow and Jack Frickel, who were "just awesome," and who paced the Locomotives to state tournament berths in 1967 and 1968.

"Obviously, he (Peterson) had seen exactly what Tom was going to be. Yay for him for picking that talent, and Tom was the best. He was the best talent and best person – just an awesome person," Spoon said.

Still, Perrigo's peers were puzzled by the attention he got from the veteran Trainman mentor, starting long before high school.

"Peterson picked him. Peterson came down and recruited the grade-school players. There was no question if you were playing basketball in Laurel in grade school, you knew he was watching," Spoon said.

Peterson "plucked" Perrigo from the grade-school ranks and designated him as someone worth developing as a future Laurel High School player, according to Spoon.

"We all kind of looked at each other and went, 'Tom?' Tom was gangly and he was just growing."

Perrigo blossomed into an all-state player his junior year and earned that honor again as a senior. He attracted the attention of Montana State University basketball coach Roger Craft, who was trying to recruit a "dream team," an all-star cast of Montana players capable of winning the Big Sky Conference title and more.

"Bozeman (MSU) had the five best players to come out of Montana in a decade or two," Spoon recalled. Besides Perrigo, Craft pulled in Koelzer, who had powered Holy Rosary to the 1969 State Class C championship; Mark Beckwith, who had made Columbia Falls a Big 32 power; Willie Weeks, who with his brother John led the Wolf Point Wolves to the 1968 State Big 32 title; and Zoonie McLean, a two-sport star from Plentywood, who besides basketball played football and earned All-Big Sky honors as MSU's quarterback in 1972. (To this day, some avid Montana prep basketball observers maintain that Willie Weeks was Montana's all-time greatest high school player.)

For Perrigo, MSU seemed a good fit. His father, Harry Perrigo, had played football in Bozeman a couple of decades before.[11] This was after the senior Perrigo, along with George Michotte, paced the then-Class A Billings Broncs – there was only one public high school in Billings until Billings West opened in the early 1960s – to the 1942 all-state basketball championship with a 48-38 win over Class B winner Klein.

"I went to MSU because my dad was a football star (for the Bobcats), it was close to home and I was recruited by a coach, Roger Craft, who was confident of producing a truly remarkable Montana team," Perrigo said in a 2014 email from his home in Perth, Australia.

The five high school stars from every section of the Treasure State made up the "cornerstone" of Craft's plan. "He wanted to develop the ultimate Montana team and, whilst individual players develop at different rates, he had a vision that when we were juniors, we would be a national power," Perrigo said.

"Having lived under Coach Peterson's philosophy, that was very inspirational."

Perrigo impressed his fellow Bobkittens, as the MSU freshman team was nicknamed, according to Koelzer. Still living in Montana's Gallatin County almost a half-century after he graduated from high school, Koelzer said in 2015 that he and his teammates often chatted with players on teams they competed against as MSU freshmen. Some of those opposing players ended up being standouts in college Division I play; a handful reached the NBA.

The consensus, when the Bobkittens and their opponents rated the talent of players they had teamed with and competed against? Perrigo was the best, according to Koelzer.

---

11 In 1947, the senior Perrigo scored one of two Bobcat touchdowns, helping Montana State College end a 10-game losing streak with a 13-12 win over the Montana State University Grizzlies.

Not knowing that level of respect for his skills existed, Perrigo said his philosophy was simple. He played basketball because he enjoyed it, "not because I had to win."

His adjustment to college life in Bozeman suffered an early setback. Soon after signing Perrigo to his letter of intent, Craft quit or was fired. "I never knew, but the impact was significant," Perrigo said, adding that Craft's replacement, Gary Hulst, "quite frankly focused on the individual, not the team. He wanted to win at all costs, and he also really did not buy into the Montana theme."

Perrigo said he never was happy at MSU despite developing "great" friendships with Weeks and Beckwith. After his freshman year, Perrigo transferred to the University of Montana in Missoula. He dropped out of college basketball and concentrated on earning a degree in education.

He said he's never regretted that decision "except that it really disappointed my parents and my teammates, but they were incredible and understood, as parents and friends, what I had to do."

Perrigo said he spent a few years rediscovering himself, embarking on a life journey that "has been and is wonderful. I have been blessed in so many ways." Among the lifelong friends he made playing basketball, he has remained especially close to Bygren. Perrigo said they bonded starting the day that Bygren, a transfer from Powell, Wyoming, arrived at LHS as a freshman.

Some have conjectured that Perrigo quit playing college for negative reasons, such as "I was on drugs, drank too much, flunked out, etc.," he said.

None of that was true, he said.

"I was an immature young man thrown into a limelight that did not allow me to discover 'me,' the person, not the basketball player. High school in Laurel did not necessarily prepare one for university. As maturity set in, I realized there was more to life than being a basketball star," Perrigo said.

He moved to Australia in 1975, married an Australian woman and embarked on a long professional career there before semi-retiring in 2016. Thus, Perrigo pointed out, he has lived in the island continent for more of his life "than my beloved Montana."

CHAPTER 20

Laurel's year after

The Locomotives' heyday did not end on March 15, 1969, when they topped Kalispell and claimed the State Big 32 championship with a 26-0 record.

The following season, 1969-70, started in promising fashion. Despite losing all five senior starters, Coach Don Peterson's squad still had Ready, the standout sophomore guard who had come off the bench several times to make a game-changing difference. The Locomotives also regained the services of a player as talented as anyone on the state championship team.

That was Flagler. Two years earlier, as a sophomore, he had been a standout on the Laurel team that qualified for the state tournament. Flagler's play brought him outstanding-sophomore-player honors in a vote of sportswriters who covered the 1968 tournament at the MSU Fieldhouse.

Then misfortune struck. Flagler took a high-low hit when tackled in preseason football practice in late summer 1968. The impact shattered his left knee, and the Locomotives lost Flagler's services at quarterback that fall. He didn't heal in time to play basketball when the Locomotives rolled to glory.

So Laurel entered the post-championship season with continued high hopes. The Locomotives hadn't lost since AA powerhouse

Great Falls topped them by a point in Saturday morning, loser-out play at the 1968 State Big 32 tournament.

Yet, almost all the familiar names, the players who had taken the Locomotives to the top of Montana high school basketball's mountain, were gone. Graduated and starting the next phase of their lives were cousins Lee Perrigo and Tom Perrigo, Campbell, Schmidt, Metzger, Spoon, Brinkel, Peterson, Clint Rooley, Bygren, Mike Belinak and Seelye.

A different change was at hand. The Big 32 no longer existed, its members having disbanded the combined Class AA-A league. Now, the state's largest high schools competed for postseason basketball honors in the new Big 16. The second tier of the former Big 32, the Class A schools, comprised the new Little 16, which included Laurel.

The 1969-70 season opened with a harbinger. In the first statewide sportswriters power poll, Laurel and Whitefish tied for the No. 1 ranking among the Little 16/Class A teams.

Though they had been bumped down a class, it wasn't as if Peterson's crew had lost its giant-killing nature.

The Locomotives opened the year-after season by whipping Big 16 foe Great Falls Central twice. Avenging their bitter 1968 state tournament loss, they tacked on a 61-60 win over the Great Falls Bison, an early season favorite to win the Big 16 championship. Trailing 35-26 at halftime, Laurel trimmed the deficit to three, 45-42, going into the fourth quarter, and the Locomotives won on Whitney's 10-foot jumper with three seconds left. That gave the Locos a symbolic triumph in light of Great Falls' previous defeat of Laurel.

Beating the Bison pushed the Locomotives' win streak to 29. They notched No. 30 the next night, a 54-48 win over Big 16 foe Great Falls Russell. Losing two starters, Steve Michael and Stan Tuomi, to injury in two nights underscored Laurel's resilience and Peterson's continued brilliance at deploying his players in roles. As before, the

Locomotives placed little or no emphasis on stardom, and capable replacements for injured starters were almost always available.

For their four wins over Big 16 schools, pollsters rewarded the Locomotives with a No. 1 ranking in the Little 16.

Now Laurel could see on the distant horizon a once-unimaginable feat: equaling or breaking the state record 56-game winning streak that the legendary Mike Lewis-led Spartans of Missoula had fashioned from 1963 to 1965. Lewis paced what was then Missoula County High School – and later Missoula Sentinel after Missoula Hellgate opened its doors – to 49 consecutive wins. Then, after Lewis graduated and enrolled at Duke University (where he became an All-American before earning a degree and playing as a professional for several years in the American Basketball Association), his former teammates tacked on seven more wins before Columbia Falls ended the streak in January 1965.

The Spartans' run of dominance included an undefeated, state championship season during the Big 32's inaugural 1963-64 season. No other unbeaten team won the Big 32 title until Laurel in 1969. Thus, the Spartans and the Locomotives became the bookends for a historic, crowd-pleasing era of Montana high school basketball.

The opportunity for Laurel's 31st straight win came on December 6, 1969, at one of the most challenging gyms in the state for visiting teams: the Golden Bears' den at Billings West. The Locomotives had won their last game with the Bears, a convincing 70-47 victory at the 1968 State Big 32 championship. This time, though, West prevailed, 49-44, to notch its 57th home victory in 65 games.

A packed house saw the lead change 26 times before Darrell Devitt streaked down the lane and passed to Paul McClure. He drained a short jumper to give the Golden Bears the lead with 3:40 left, and Mike Loken iced the win with two free throws.

For Ready, West's streak-ending win over his Locomotives still stands out among the many down-to-the-wire games he played in the purple and gold uniform of Laurel.

Asked, though, to recall anything memorable in the West-Laurel contest, Ready hesitated.

"It's hard to. It's like you've been in so many close ones over the years. That one didn't come through," he said more than four decades later.

"It's disappointing. You think you're never going to lose but then it happens."

Despite the loss to West, the graduation-depleted Locomotives got an early boost from their continued success against larger schools (in terms of enrollment or player size or both). Notching four wins in two weekends against squads such as that resulted in "a good feeling" and gave the Locomotives a sense they could carry on the legacy established by the previous year's team, Ready said.

Noting Flagler's return to the form that had made him a sophomore star, Ready said the 1969-70 team was ready to make its own mark.

"It was a good feeling; it was a continuation. We were starting fresh, working as a new team. Everybody got on the same team as (coach Don) Peterson," he said.

December 1969, though, set the tone for an up-and-down year, unlike the long, undefeated run the Locomotives experienced the season before.

The loss to Billings West began a four-game losing streak that closed out the calendar year. Laurel traveled to Lewistown, another Big 16 member, and suffered a 63-51 setback highlighted by the Golden Eagles' sizable rebounding edge.

Then came the matchup that hadn't materialized at the state tournament in Bozeman the previous March: Wolf Point, the 1968 State Big 32 champion, versus the reigning champion Locomotives.

They traveled to northeastern Montana to face the Wolves and absorbed a turnover-plagued 60-49 defeat. Still, Peterson's crew left with a couple of bright spots: Flagler's 14 points and Ready's free throw accuracy – he converted five straight attempts and ran his streak to 17 in a row.

Laurel traveled an hour's drive west for the next night's game against the Glasgow Scotties, who tagged a 57-44 loss on the Locomotives. Behind by five points early in the fourth quarter, the Scotties outscored the Locos, 21-4, in the frame to pull away. Flagler and Ready tallied 16 points each, but Ready's free-throw streak ended at 17 when he missed his first try of the game.

The Locomotives got back on the winning track by beating Miles City, 55-49, in Laurel's first game of 1970, but Peterson's crew fell to Hardin, 58-52, the next night.

The Locomotives rebounded by beating Sidney and Glendive and then avenging the loss to Wolf Point with a one-point win over the Wolves at home. In that game, Flagler poured in 24 points and Ready got 12. Whitney, a reserve for the Locomotives the year before, tossed in 14 points.

The Locomotives lost again to Glasgow, whipped Miles City and fell to arch-rival Billings Central on the Laurel court. Then came four Laurel wins to close out the regular season, giving the Locomotives a 14-6 season record (10-4 in the Little 16) going into the divisional tournament on their court.

Laurel opened the postseason by edging Glendive before a capacity crowd of 3,000, but their nemesis – Glasgow – showed up next. The Scotties won the semifinal matchup by seven points, sending the Locomotives into loser-out play. They recovered to whip Wolf Point, 76-60, and they notched a second win in Saturday play, edging Sidney for third place and a berth at the state tournament.

The Little 16 state tournament that year took place at what then was the Eastern Montana College Fieldhouse. (EMC has since become Montana State University Billings.)

The Locomotives trimmed Anaconda Central (one of several Catholic high schools in the state that later closed due to funding shortages) and then avenged three earlier losses to Glasgow, edging the Scotties, 47-45, in a contest highlighted by two crucial free throws from sophomore Byron Spoon (Dan's younger brother) with 1:04 left.

That put Laurel into the championship game against Whitefish, the northwestern Montana squad with which the Locomotives had shared the pre-season No. 1 ranking. The Bulldogs broke Laurel's full-court press and used a 54-35 rebounding advantage to cruise to a 54-44 win. Wayne Weischaar, another Laurel sophomore, tallied 15 points.

Assistant coach Tom Wilson pinpointed Laurel's problem in the finale. "It was just too much for one senior to carry," he told the *Billings Gazette,* referring to Flagler's starring role on a team where other starters and reserves were all juniors and sophomores.

Still, the Locomotives finished the 1969-70 season with a fine 19-8 record and another piece of state tournament hardware to add to the school's trophy case. Laurel's youngsters had gained experience and were ready for another run to glory.

Again, in 1971, the Locomotives found themselves in the bridesmaid role. They reached the Class A state championship game but fell to long time Eastern Montana rival Sidney, 67-60.

Laurel returned to the pinnacle of Montana prep basketball. In 1972, the Locomotives capped a sparkling, near-perfect 25-1 season by capturing the state title with a 47-44 win over Hamilton. Laurel overcame a 22-9 deficit in the second quarter, trailed by four at halftime and pulled into a tie at 35 as the third quarter ended. Capping a fine career, Weischaar led Laurel with 12 points.

By then, it was a new cast, albeit with a few familiar last names: Byron Spoon and Pat Belinak, younger brothers of Dan Spoon and Mike Belinak. Rounding out Peterson's second state championship team were Richard Hanks, Steve Barrett, Rick Dietrich, Lon Frickel, Dan Williams, Ed Neibauer, Duane Kroll, Jack Gabrian and Rick Southworth.

CHAPTER 21

The Laurel legacy

1969 represented a breakthrough for the Locomotives, the first state basketball championship, boys or girls in at least 55 years that Laurel High School played the sport on an interscholastic basis.[12]

Forty-seven years later, Seelye, the senior forward whose deadly medium-range shooting helped the Locomotives surmount the title hurdle, continues to have positive sentiments about what the team accomplished in the final divisional and state Big 32 tournaments.

"It was a lot of fun," he said, and Laurel received "a lot of notoriety" as the capital of Montana high school basketball in 1969.

"We were almost like celebrities in town for a while after that," he said, adding that felt relief when the season finished.

Seelye, however, is wistful. How good were he and the rest of the Locomotives compared with their prep peers of that era? "We thought too bad they don't have regionals and nationals because we thought could do well," he said.

---

12 The earliest references to Laurel playing interscholastic basketball found by the author are from 1914: Big Timber dedicated a new gym by playing host to Laurel, defeating the visitors, 42-23. *Anaconda Standard*, January 11, 1914. Laurel was among the high schools expected to play in the 1914 state basketball tournament, scheduled in early March that year in Bozeman. *Anaconda Standard*, February 19, 1914.

That didn't happen. With the Big 32 disbanded, the Locomotives again competed in the Class A ranks, the same stage they had played in before 1964. Three years after winning the state crown, with Montana using a Big 16 (Class AA) and Little 16 (Class A) setup for the largest high schools, Don Peterson guided the Locos to their second state title.

That 1972 Laurel team captured the crown by beating Hamilton, 47-44, in the tournament in Butte. The Locomotives finished the year with the second-best record in school history, 25-1.

In the period between the first two state titles, the Locomotives stayed among the state Class A elite. They reached the state title game in both 1970 and 1971, losing to champs Whitefish and Sidney.

Then it was a long wait for a third state boys crown. Not that the Locomotives didn't come close.

Health issues prompted Peterson to retire from teaching at Laurel in the late 1970s. He and his wife, Dorothy, moved to Great Falls and then to the northwest Montana resort community of Bigfork. There, Peterson devoted much of his working time to what had been a summer job for him and coaching colleagues: roaming the state as a crop insurance adjuster, employed by a company in neighboring Kalispell.

Peterson, however, got one more taste of guiding young athletes on the hardwood. He came out of retirement to coach Class B Bigfork's boys team in 1994-95.

One of Peterson's assistants when he coached Bigfork was a former player, Jerry Bygren, the steady center on the 1969 title team. Bygren got a basketball scholarship to attend Concordia College in Minnesota. He played there two years, then transferred to the University of Montana, and ended his competitive basketball play except for intramural participation. After college, he came to

Bigfork, was hired by a local bank and became its long time president.

Peterson retired for good in 1996; as of 2016, he was one of three Montana high school boys coaches to reach the 500-win mark.

Meanwhile, his immediate successor at Laurel, Alan Campbell, one of the 1969 headline players, took over the reins for several years. He got the Locomotives into Saturday night play at a couple state Class A tournaments but couldn't pull off the big win. Campbell next had a short stint coaching his original high school, Billings Central, then moved to Texas where he continued his teaching and coaching career in El Paso. His final stop was in the West Texas town of Merkel, where he taught but did not coach.

Long wait ends

It took 38 years, until 2010, before Laurel claimed another state boys title. That year, Pat Hansen guided the Locomotives to the championship with a 60-48 win over Polson at the finals in Butte.

Hansen had coached the Gardner Bruins to the 2005 State Class A championship. He took Laurel to the top in his fifth year in the rail town.

After the 2010 championship, Hansen acknowledged what he inherited from his predecessors at Laurel: Peterson, Campbell and Bruce Robertson.

"Saturday's championship was a great win for us, but it was also a win for the coaches, players and fans that have been waiting for the past 38 years for another state championship," Hansen told the *Laurel Outlook*.

"Laurel is a great basketball town," he said.

Hansen proved prescient. He took just five years to win his second state title in Laurel.

The 2015 Locomotives took top honors in the Worthington Arena of what is now called the Brick Breeden Fieldhouse at

Montana State University. They claimed their fourth boys state crown with a masterful 61-52 win over Dillon.

Going into the tournament, Dillon was the odds-on favorite. The Beavers won the state football championship in November 2014 with one of the most talented assemblages of athletes ever seen in Class A. Most of those players changed over to basketball in late November. The Beavers reeled off 19 straight wins to reach their date with Laurel in Bozeman on March 14, 2015 – exactly one day short of 46 years after the Locomotives epic overtime win against Kalispell at the same venue.

Laurel, meanwhile, didn't appear to be championship caliber. Earlier in the season (January 16, 2015), the Locomotives suffered a 36-30 home-court loss to Eastern A rival Glendive. It was the Locos' fourth loss in five games.

"We had a tough stretch there," guard Brandon Kubitz told *Billings Gazette* sportswriter Greg Rachac in an article published the day after the state tournament.

"As a team we sat in the locker room, we talked it out, we talked about how we could do better and what we needed to be doing.

"We told ourselves that if we do all that and count on the coaching staff and the people around us, we're going to end up right there with a chance to win the state championship. "

In Bozeman, Laurel held off first-game draw Belgrade, 48-46. Then came what Rachac described as the Locos' kryptonite: the state semifinal game. On four consecutive occasions (2011-2014), Hansen's squads had won their first state tournament game only to lose on Friday night.

Not this time. Cooper Love swished a game-opening three-pointer, and the Locomotives led from start to finish for a 58-55 victory over Butte Central.

Against Dillon, Laurel played lights-out defense that would have made the late Don Peterson proud, combined with a productive half-court offense. The Locomotives shot 70 percent from the field in the first half of both the championship game and the semifinal game. They cooled off only slightly in the second half against Dillon, finishing with 68-percent accuracy.

Tyler Thompson led the Locos with 18 points on 5-for-6 field-goal shooting. Just as important, Laurel got 10 points from reserves Marshall Simanton, Hayden Love and Shay Osborne, which was enough to win. Their output offset having starter Zac Allen benched for a long stretch because of foul trouble.

When the nets were cut and the trophy held high, players encircled by jubilant Laurel fans, the Locomotives could look back on a strong finish to the 2015 season: 14 wins in their final 16 games.

Past inspires present

Several weeks after the championship, Hansen wove the 2015 team's accomplishment into a tapestry spanning the years since Peterson, Campbell and Robertson filled his role.

"That's one thing I really try to do in Laurel, is to bring the history back into it," he said in a May 2015 interview.

"We have stars on our uniforms and warm-ups – Don Peterson always put stars on stuff.

"And we had different Laurel signature things put on when Bruce Robertson was through. So we try to bring back that history of it.

"My son's godparents are Mike and Barb Belinak; Mike was on that '69 team. And Leon Schmidt (a member of the '69 team who retired from an out-of-state job and returned to Laurel) was a (school) bus driver this year. He was on that '69 team."

In 2010, the Locomotives and Hanson received a symbol of the continuity between their squad and players on Peterson's Big 32 championship team. Belinak still had his miniature gold basketball, something that each player received after the 1969 win over

Kalispell. Belinak had 2010 engraved on his basketball and gave it to Hansen.

"I have that in a little case," Hansen said.

"Alan Campbell sent video ... of the '69 game, audio of it and (video from) some of the home games (in 1968-69).

"I just love it. I have one of Peterson's playbooks. I thumb through it once in a while. I think it's pretty neat."

Schmidt praised Hansen's coaching ability, comparing him with another coach who has joined college football's elite: Ohio State's Urban Meyer, who guided the Buckeyes to the 2015 BCS championship and also led Florida to national championships in 2006 and 2008. Schmidt got a first-hand look at Meyer's coaching prowess when both were in Utah, Schmidt as an employee in Salt Lake City of a check printing company while Meyer was at the helm of the University of Utah in 2003 and 2004.

In 2004, Meyer led the undefeated Utes to a Bowl Championship Series bid, something that had not been done by a team from a non-automatically qualifying BCS conference since the formation of the BCS in 1998. He coached Utah to a Fiesta Bowl win over Pittsburgh, capping the Utes' first perfect season (12–0) since 1930. That accomplishment earned Meyer national coach of the year honors and prompted a job offer from Florida that he accepted.

"Pat Hansen has that same quality and direction and coaching ability that I saw in Urban Meyer. He's just that good a coach where like they said, we're going to change things up a little bit and this is my game plan. You give me two weeks to work on it, and we're gonna be there," Schmidt said.

Laurel's four state championships put the Locomotives in elite company, just behind the Class A leaders in that category: Miles City, eight; Sidney, six, including an all-time state record four in a row from 1957-1960; and Glendive and Butte Central, five each.

Another Hansen-coached school, Gardiner, shows up in the record books for consecutive wins. The 2004-05 Bruins rank fifth on that list with 36 wins. Laurel officially is No. 7 with 30 in a row from 1968-70, although neighboring Park City won 31 straight from 1969 to 1971 (including a 28-0 state championship run in 1970). Park City doesn't appear on the honor roll because school administrators apparently overlooked sending in the required paperwork to the Montana High School Association.

Hanson has reached elite company among his coaching peers for something else. He's among a group tied for fourth place all-time with three state championships each. Toby Kangas and Robert Lowry lead with six state titles. All of Lowry's came during his tenure at Wolf Point. Kangas split his titles evenly between Sidney and Billings West.

Hansen also has entered another select group: those Montana coaches with state titles in more than one class. Retired coach Pat O'Connor stands alone atop the list with championships in three classes – C (Park City), A (Glendive), and AA (Billings Senior). Hansen is one of seven coaches to win state championships in two classes.

CHAPTER 22

Don Peterson: the coach and the man

Don Peterson's coaching career spanned five decades. In that time, he interacted with students and players from the schools where he taught and coached, plus many players and coaches from other schools that competed against Peterson's teams. Ask them to describe him nowadays, and you'll get a wide range of comments, nearly all laudatory, although Peterson's complex personality caused at least one former player to praise his coaching brilliance while saying he fell short in interpersonal relationships.

One competing player, Curt LeRossignol, formed memories of Peterson as a star for a powerful rival of the Locomotives, the Livingston Rangers. LeRossignol was a 6-7 senior forward for the Rangers in 1967-68. After graduation, he was awarded an athletic scholarship to the University of Nebraska, where his grandfather had founded the school of business. He played on the Cornhuskers' freshman team when first-year players weren't allowed to play varsity ball. He lettered for the Huskers in 1971-72.

LeRossignol, now a real estate developer in Denver, remembers one unusual aspect of Peterson's coaching. It appeared in March 1968, when the Locomotives defeated the favored Rangers in a Monday night challenge game at the Big 32 Division One tournament in Great Falls. The win gave Laurel a berth at the state tournament in Bozeman.

The anecdote, first mentioned by Laurel players and expanded upon by LeRossignol, involved a minor embarrassment he endured during the challenge game. LeRossignol suspects but is not sure to this day that Laurel's Tom Perrigo was the perpetrator – and that Peterson instigated the event. (Other former Laurel players say the perpetrator may have been Bygren.)

"We creamed 'em in Livingston and beat 'em in Laurel, so we were shocked about the divisional (tournament loss to the Locomotives)," LeRossignol said in January 2015.

"I remember pretty distinctly. I thought he (Perrigo) was pinching me in the ass," he said. The way the Laurel players tell the story, one of them tried to grab LeRossignol's trunks and pull them down.

LeRossignol said he swung around and gave the Laurel player, whoever it might have been, "a light elbow in the face."

"They threw me out of the game," he said. "I just got so upset. I'm not going to pin it on Perrigo; it was a Laurel Locomotive," LeRossignol said, however, he holds nothing against the Laurel team.

Peterson "was such a crafty coach. I wonder if he put them up to it," LeRossignol said.

Proving that there was no lasting hard feeling, LeRossignol sent Peterson a handwritten letter from Lincoln, Nebraska, on March 9, 1969 (during the week between the Big 32 divisional and Big 32 state tournaments). "I just wanted to congratulate you and your team on an excellent season so far and to wish you all the luck in the world at the state tourney this week," he wrote.

The then college freshman said it might "sound strange" to have a former Livingston player writing to encourage one of his school's top rivals, "but you have had a great season. I just wish ours could have ended on a bit of a more happy note last year. I often think back to our game with your team and replay it – but the funny thing is, it keeps coming out the same way. That is the way the ball bounces, I guess – and all the way down the road you have to take the losses as well as the victories in stride."

Houtenon, the Great Falls guard whose Bison squad knocked the Locomotives out of the 1968 state tournament, is someone else who admired Peterson's ability to maximize performance from players who often were shorter and seemingly less talented than their rivals.

Houtenon grew up in Great Falls next door to Gerry Hall, who moved to Kalispell when he was about 12 and became a starting guard on the Braves' 1969 state runner-up team. Houtenon and Hall later became brothers-in-law.

In 2015, Houtenon recalled a recent conversation he had with Hall.

"I said, 'I know you played on that team with Brent Wilson. OK, how come you guys lost that game?'

"He said, 'Coach Peterson, he's a pretty crafty fellow. He took Lee Perrigo, who was absolutely their most slow-footed guard. They went into kind of a half-assed zone, and they put Lee Perrigo down in front of Wilson. He fronted him all day long. Every time Wilson would go to make a move for the ball, he'd fall over Perrigo and he'd get called for a foul,' " Houtenon said.

That foul trouble – Wilson was benched for part of the second half and fouled out with seconds to go in regulation play – helped Laurel seal its three-point win over Kalispell.

Another renowned Montana prep coach credits some of his success to Peterson's tutelage.

"He was a good friend," said Tom Ferch, who steered the high-powered, run-and-gun Livingston Rangers to state Class A championships in 1983 and 1985. Ferch, now retired, lives in Bozeman.

"Here's how I met Don," Ferch said in 2016. He had been coaching in Alaska before he returned to the Treasure State; Ferch is a native of the Eastern Montana town of Circle. Plenty Coups High School, an all-Indian school in the town of Pryor on the Crow Reservation south of Billings, had just opened. Ferch became the Warriors' first boys basketball coach in the mid-1970s.

"I knew Don was one of the best coaches in the state. I called him up and said, 'Hey, I want to pick your brains a little bit,'" Ferch said.

Peterson replied, "Yeah, come on over. Class is out about 3:30." Ferch made the short drive from Pryor to Laurel in time for the final bell.

"I saw down in a student desk and he set up a blackboard and started showing me some stuff. And then he'd come to our Plenty Coups games because we got to be good friends."

Ferch recalled Peterson coming to the Metra in Billings to watch the Warriors play in a post-season tournament. "We won it. He came down and said, 'Helluva coaching job, Tom.' I'll always remember that – that was 40 years ago."

Peterson's high school basketball coaching skills, perhaps bordering on genius, cannot be doubted or disputed. He won 558 games during his career, second-most in Montana boys prep history. He's a member of the Montana Coaches Hall of Fame, and also for reaching the 500-win threshold has been honored at the Naismith Hall of Fame in Springfield, Massachusetts. There, he joined other high school coaches around the U.S. who have achieved that plateau.

Letdown for two seniors

Describing Peterson completely, though, brings out a more nuanced picture, one of an intelligent individual who sometimes had difficulty dealing with the psyches of his teenage charges. His relationship with two senior reserve players, Dan Spoon and Clint Rooley, illustrates Peterson's complex personality.

Spoon, a 5-10 senior guard on Laurel's championship team, made the varsity as a junior. So he played behind standouts like Jack Frickel and Bob Crow, who paced the Locomotives to a berth in the 1968 State Big 32 tournament. Spoon also took the court alongside Kevin Flagler, a young standout in 1968 who was a starting guard by late season and who sportswriters and sportscasters called the Treasure State's top sophomore player at the state tournament that year.

Spoon, now a lawyer in Missoula who also ranches near Helena, had reason to think, as he awaited his senior year in high school, that he'd contribute to a team with the potential to be among the state's elite. He had put in endless hours of practice time, had started occasionally, and knew the Locomotives system – the "Peterson Way" instilled in Laurel boys starting in about the third grade when their coaches showed them the basic offensive and defensive sets Peterson preached.

"Basketball was not only my life; it was my sanctuary. I grew up in a house that was hugely dysfunctional. So I'm a block away from the junior high and every day, I'm down there playing with the big kids."

Frickel and Crow had graduated, but the Locomotives had a roster dominated by senior returnees with game experience, plus an outstanding junior in Flagler.

"We were geared for the '69 season, without (transfers Alan) Campbell and Lee (Perrigo), to be pretty danged good," Spoon recalled in 2016.

The first setback came in late summer 1968 when Flagler, the Locomotives' certain starting quarterback, shattered his knee in pre-season football practice and was lost for both football and basketball.

Then, when basketball practice started in November, Spoon realized that his expectations of ample playing time – even perhaps starting – for Laurel his senior year didn't match reality. Looking back now, he said he's thankful for the addition of Campbell and Perrigo to the team. Yet it's thankfulness mixed with recollection of disappointment.

"Those guys obviously made us better, but there was a lot of luck involved, a lot of camaraderie. There were a lot of interesting dynamics," he said.

Though, as a 17-year-old, Spoon had trouble handling the new realities, he acknowledges now, as an adult in his mid-60s, the conflict between his expectations and reality. "I worked my ass off and, yeah, so it's my turn," was his mind set, which collided with his coach's plans.

"These other elements come into play. What's happening?" he said, recalling is thoughts almost five decades later. "I was right there in the mix, like I thought I would be." But it became clear that Spoon would mostly sit on the Locos' bench, not start. "It was very disappointing that that happened," he said.

Even today, Spoon says he was hurt by not getting the playing time he thought he had earned. "It was a very big deal to me," he said.

He explained the "critically important" team dynamics. "Peterson was a genius for basketball X's and O's." Plus, "He was way ahead of his time in terms of our gear. We had Adidas shoes. Nobody wore those; everybody wore Converse."

"We had warm-ups that had our names on the back of them." and the Locomotives went through Harlem Globetrotters-style pregame routines to the strains of their pep band playing "Sweet Georgia Brown."

All that made a psychological impression on opponents visiting the Laurel gym. "All of a sudden, all of these teams come in and say, 'Holy shit, this is a really well-organized (program).' We were. We had that dynamic," Spoon said.

Peterson was an "exceptional" coach and a master at making his teams feel special. "What he was not exceptional at was interpersonal relationships. Thank God for (assistant coach) Karl Fiske, who was my sounding board," Spoon said. "He kept me as calm as I possibly could be." Fiske told Spoon and others who had occasional difficulties with Peterson's style that "you're going to be champions – you just have to bide your time and do what you're asked to do."

Spoon remembers another game – he's not sure which one – where he apparently set a state record for the shortest amount of time played.

"I was in for the first free throw (and pulled) out for the second of a two-shot foul," a substitution now illegal under game rules.

"That's how far I'd come, from starting to not getting any time. It was embarrassing."

Looking back more than four decades later, Spoon said his coach was a mathematical genius. "This guy, after every game ... would do these little triangular pieces of wood with 'Dan Spoon,' five assists, 14 points. He would hand these things out with a pat on the back for everybody.[13]

"Statistics were hugely important to him. But he couldn't communicate," Spoon said.

Spoon adopted a different style when he got a chance to coach years later. He coached in an AAU basketball program in Missoula and took his son and daughter, along with teammates, on trips to summer camps in Montana, Wyoming and Idaho. Both of Spoon's children became starters as sophomores at Missoula Sentinel High School, and his son, Danny, a two-time all-stater, was Montana's top

---

13 The diamond-shaped wooden awards were made by the school's Art Club as a fund-raising activity. Most players liked them, according to Ric Peterson, and he said his mother still has his award.

scorer in 1998 when he was named the best prep player in the state. Both children also played college basketball.

"I've been consumed by the sport," Spoon said. "What you learn after all that time is basketball is a confidence game, and Pete didn't engender confidence.

"One size does not fit all. There are kids you need to kick 'em in the ass to get them going; there are kids you need to put your arms around and say, this is not the way you do it."

Some players need regular pats on the back, something Peterson didn't seem to grasp, according to Spoon. He said Fiske, who doubled as head football coach, taught geometry and was already a grandfather when he worked with the 1969 team, filled the gap.

Spoon said Fiske was "an aw shucks kind of guy. (He was the) nicest human being I've ever encountered in my lifetime. He was the salt of the earth ... the glue that kept everybody together."

Peterson's brilliance was evident in tactical basketball matters such as his famed modified stratified, switching zone defenses. Throw in Fiske's ability to read teenage players' emotional ups and downs, add his calming influence when needed, and the result was a "combination of a lot of good things," Spoon said.

In testimony to his coach's tactical brilliance, Spoon said that when he coached, "I used Pete's offense."

Clint Rooley's situation further illustrates the complex team dynamics that Peterson managed during the 1968-69 season. Peterson carried the slender 6-1 senior guard on the roster throughout the regular season.

That was based on sound reasoning, according to Ric Peterson. Rooley was the team's best jumper, which helped at times such as the road game against Miles City when he came in to counter the Cowboys.

Rooley held the basketball try outs screening record for vertical jump and he was a track standout who held the school record in high jump for many years, Peterson recalled.

As state tournament time approached, though, Don Peterson faced a difficult decision. Should he keep the senior on the state tournament squad, with a roster limited to 12 players by Montana High School Association rules? Or, should he go with Ready, the talented sophomore whose clutch shooting had helped Laurel escape tough spots in the Lewistown and Great Falls Russell games?

Peterson lobbied the MHSA to change tournament rules to allow replacements for injured players, according to Ric Peterson. In hindsight, Laurel would have benefited in 1969 had Rooley been available to replace Schmidt after he was injured in the semifinal game. The rule, though, never changed.

So, Peterson picked Ready, which made the day or two before the tournament difficult for the Trainmen mentor.

"Clint was quite a scrappy competitor. My dad like Clint and was near tears after his phone call with Clint's parents when the final cut was announced," Ric Peterson said.

Out of the limelight

Few people saw a side of Don Peterson different from the on-court basketball coaching genius. Yet, something besides an urge to compete at the highest level prompted Peterson to lend his skills outside regular avenues later in his career. The episode came to light years afterward during a memorial service for Don Peterson in the spring of 2003, according to Peterson's oldest son and close confidant Ric. Family members and friends had gathered in the Laurel High School gym to pay tribute to Peterson after his death at age 76.

One of those who spoke was Bob Deming, a friend and teaching colleague of Peterson's who also played fast-pitch softball with him when both were young men.

After Peterson's "first" retirement from LHS (he later coached two years in Bigfork, Montana), he worked for Crop Hail Management as field office director in Great Falls. There, he resumed his friendship with Deming.

At the memorial service, Deming related a chapter in Don Peterson's life that helps explains a discrepancy in Peterson's reported career win total. The Montana High School Association web site credits him with 546 wins, but most Montana newspaper articles written since the early 2000s show him with 12 more wins, 558.[14]

Deming said at the 2003 event that some of Peterson's early coaching wins may not have been reported to the MHSA because they occurred in an unofficial capacity, Ric Peterson said.

"There were more wins that weren't counted because when my dad was manning the crop insurance office in Great Falls, he helped coach the state school (Montana School for the Deaf and Blind) to several wins. Bob Deming asked him to come and assist because those kids were just getting pummeled. They played a regular Class C schedule and he won games there. He turned them around."

The younger Peterson said he first learned of his father's moonlight coaching from Deming's posthumous tribute.

Proof in the pudding

Still, Peterson's standing in the top ranks of Montana prep coaches is guaranteed, according to someone who got to know him early in a 50-year reporting career. That's Clarke, who was sports editor of

---

14 Peterson's 558 career wins, against 250 losses, spanned a 33-year coaching career at six schools, Florence-Carlton, Frenchtown, two times at Belt, Augusta, Laurel and Bigfork. "West: defense was key to Peterson's title teams," Billings Gazette, June 25, 2003.

the Billings Gazette from 1968 through the early 1970s. Remembering Peterson in a 2014 interview, Clarke said he seemed a soft-spoken person who got impressive results from his teams.

"I think he has to go down as one of the top three coaches in Montana history," Clarke said.

What Peterson did in 1968-69 stands out "as one of the great accomplishments in coaching history," Clarke said.

"It wasn't fluky. If you go through it, look at those scores, of those 26 games, in 15, Laurel held the opponents to 50 or less points."

Facing the best of Montana's Class AA and A teams in the combined Big 32 classification, Peterson's Locomotives held opponents to an average 51 points a game, while averaging 66 themselves, which Clarke called a remarkable achievement.

"You're basically saying, 'We're going to first beat you on defense and then we're going to be good enough to score more points than you.'"

Clarke remembers Peterson, above all, as a "no-nonsense guy."

"He wasn't one of those guys who'd be tough to talk to after a loss," he said. "He was a gentleman – one of my favorite people. I never saw anything from him that came off as a guy with a lot of ego."

Clarke said Peterson never was a "screamer," trying to motivate his player with histrionics. Instead, the style of New England Patriots coach Bill Belichick comes to mind in Clarke's opinion.

"I think he was one of those Belichick guys that saw things and imparted that knowledge and players believed in so much," he said.

Those in Montana's coaching and sports writing ranks saw evidence of the effectiveness of Peterson's approach in the record he compiled as one of three Treasure State coaches to accumulate 500-plus wins.

"The proof is in the pudding," Clarke said.

CHAPTER 23

Big game over for two teenagers

March 15, 1969. 10 p.m.

The game was over. Jubilant Laurel fans surrounded their triumphant Locomotives, who hoisted the big trophy high for all to see. Chants of "We're No. 1!" swept through the throng.

I sat at the courtside press table, inside the Montana State University Fieldhouse. A 17-year-old high school senior hoping to launch a career in sports writing, I tried to soak up as many memories and impressions as possible. Little did I know that this game would become an epic in Montana sports history, one of the most memorable I'd see or cover for the Billings Gazette or any of the other three newspapers for which I reported or served as editor.

I noticed a solitary figure on the floor about 10 feet away from me. He was unmistakable. Brent Wilson, all 6-foot-11 of him, towered over everyone. I don't remember if he said anything. If he did, I was too far away and there was too much noise to hear him.

What I'll never forget, though, was Brent standing there, by himself, shaking his head. That said everything. *I can't believe it.*

But the Locomotives and their loyal fans? They believed. They had won 'em all.

APPENDIX A

1968-69 season summary

Regular-season play

December 1968

No. 1: Laurel 76, Lovell, Wyoming, 57

Date: December 6, 1968; Location: Lovell, Wyoming.

Guard Alan Campbell and forward Lee Perrigo combined for 44 points, powering the Locomotives to an easy season-opening win over Lovell.

The nonconference game saw Laurel race to a 25-8 first-quarter lead and pad the margin to 43-21 at halftime. The Locomotives continued to control the game after intermission, going up, 64-36, after three quarters.

Laurel emptied its bench during the fourth quarter.

Campbell scored 26 points, and Perrigo added 18.

Laurel scoring summary: Campbell 26, T. Perrigo 18, Dan Spoon 6, Lee Perrigo 7, Roger Seelye 5, Jerry Bygren 5, Leon Schmidt 7, Mark Metzger 2.

No. 2: Laurel 83, Cody, Wyoming, 63

Date: December 7, 1968; Location: Cody, Wyoming

Cody grabbed a two-point lead at the end of the first quarter, but the Locomotives took charge in the second quarter and rolled to a comfortable victory.

Tom Perrigo scored 27 points to pace Laurel. Three teammates joined him in double figures: Leon Schmidt and Roger Seelye, with 16 each, and Alan Campbell, with 14.

Trailing 20-18 after one period, Laurel led at halftime, 41-34, and padded its lead to 59-44 after three quarters.

Laurel scoring summary: T. Perrigo 27, Schmidt 16, Seelye 16, Campbell 14, Spoon 3, L. Perrigo 3, Ric Peterson 2, Bygren 2.

No. 3: Laurel 53, Hardin 44

Date: December 13, 1968; Location: Hardin

Laurel opened Big 32 conference play with a win over the Bulldogs that was in doubt until the fourth quarter.

Laurel led at the quarter stops, 13-12, 27-21, and 37-36, but Hardin grabbed a 35-33 lead with 35 seconds left in the third quarter. The Bulldogs also nipped at the Locomotives' heels in the fourth quarter until Tom Perrigo sank four consecutive free throws for a 45-40 advantage with 3½ minutes to go.

Perrigo took game honors with 21 points. Alan Campbell added 18 points.

Laurel scoring summary: T. Perrigo 21, Seelye 9, L. Perrigo 2, Spoon 3, Campbell 18

No. 4: Laurel 57, Billings Senior 56

Date: December 18, 1968; Location: Billings Senior

Head coach Don Peterson missed this Laurel victory. He stayed home after contracting the flu, turning the coaching reins over to Karl Fiske and Tom Wilson.

All Peterson could do was listen to a radio broadcast of the game, but his assistants came through. They guided the Locomotives to a one-point win over the Broncs, who were a little more than one season removed from winning the Big 32 championship in March 1967. Laurel had not defeated the big-city school in several decades, and the win avenged a 69-49 loss to the Broncs the previous season.

It was Laurel's closest win of the season.

Laurel trailed 15-1 in the first quarter but outscored Senior, 18-5, in the second quarter for a 30-26 halftime margin.

The Locomotives, up by 49-40 with 5:30 remaining in the game, saw their lead vanish as the Broncs scored 12 unanswered points for 52-49 edge with two minutes to go. The Broncs still led, 54-51, with 1:35 remaining, but Laurel's pressing defense produced several Senior turnovers in the late going. The Broncs gave up the ball 27 times in the contest.

Two Tom Perrigo free throws put Laurel in front for good, 55-54, with 45 seconds remaining. Reserve Mark Metzger iced the win by converting two more from the line with 23 seconds to go, making it 57-54. The free throws proved crucial because Senior's Dan Pekich sank a 20-footer with six seconds left to close scoring.

Perrigo took game honors with 20 points, and Alan Campbell added 12.

Laurel scoring summary: Campbell 12, T. Perrigo 20, Spoon 2, Seelye 2, Metzger 2, Bygren 7, Schmidt 7, L. Perrigo 4.

No. 5: Laurel 66, Lewistown 49

Date: December 20, 1968; Location: Laurel

Laurel led all the way to go into the Christmas break with a perfect record. The Locomotives held leads of 19-10, 37-27 and 46-33 at the quarter stops.

Alan Campbell paced the Locomotives with 19 points, Tom Perrigo added 17, and Jerry Bygren tallied 14.

Laurel won without the services of Roger Seelye, a stalwart rebounder and scorer injured in the Billings Senior game two days earlier.

Laurel scoring summary: Campbell 19, Perrigo 17, Leon Schmidt 9, Bygren 14, Mark Metzger 2, Mike Belinak 2, Dave Brinkel 2, Lon Peterson 1.

January 1969

No. 6: Laurel 53, Miles City 42

Date: January 3, 1969; Location: Laurel

Laurel, ranked No. 4 in the state sportswriters' power poll, toppled No. 6 Miles City in a defensive battle.

The Locomotives controlled the boards against the taller Cowboys, accumulating a 48-33 rebounding margin. Jerry Bygren grabbed 13 rebounds.

Miles City pulled into a tie at 13 in the second quarter before the Locomotives took charge. They pulled ahead by nine points in the fourth quarter and widened the margin at the buzzer.

Tom Perrigo and Alan Campbell paced the Laurel offense with 16 points and 15 points, respectively.

Laurel scoring summary: Tom Perrigo 16, Roger Seelye 9, Bygren 1, Lee Perrigo 12, Campbell 15.

No. 7: Laurel 56, Hardin 34

Date: January 4, 1969; Location: Laurel

Laurel used double-figure scoring from Alan Campbell and Tom Perrigo to roll past Hardin.

Campbell poured in 15 points, and Perrigo scored 13. Perrigo also pulled down 15 rebounds.

The Locomotives led at the end of each quarter: 15-4, 24-12, and 41-21.

Laurel scoring summary: T. Perrigo 13, Roger Seelye 2, Jerry Bygren 7, Lee Perrigo 8, Campbell 15, Dan Spoon 4, Leon Schmidt 2, Mike Belinak 2, Mark Metzger 2.

No. 8: Laurel 60, Glendive 50

Date: January 10, 1969; Location: Glendive

Laurel validated its No. 3 statewide ranking by taking an early lead over Glendive and protecting it the rest of the game.

The Locomotives owned quarter leads of 18-11, 32-24, and 49-35.

Tom Perrigo picked up game scoring honors with 24 points.

No scoring summary available.

No. 9: Laurel 82, Sidney 66

Date: January 11, 1969; Location: Sidney

The Locomotives rallied from a first-quarter deficit to beat the Eagles.

Behind 23-17 after the first eight minutes, Laurel built a 38-35 halftime lead and entered the final quarter leading, 62-50.

Three Locomotives scored in double figures: Tom Perrigo, 26 points; Lee Perrigo, 18; and Alan Campbell, 16.

Laurel scoring summary: Tom Perrigo 26, Lee Perrigo 18, Dan Spoon 2, Leon Schmidt 3, Alan Campbell 16, Jerry Bygren 2, Mike Belinak 2, Roger Seelye 13.

No. 10: Laurel 60, Great Falls Central 44

Date: January 17, 1969; Location: Laurel

Laurel outrebounded the Mustangs, 59-31, and led the entire way en route to an easy victory.

The Locomotives held quarter leads of 11-6, 31-20, and 43-32.

Tom Perrigo and Roger Seelye shared scoring honors with 20 points each. Illness reduced playing time for star guard Alan Campbell.

Laurel scoring summary: Tom Perrigo 20, Jerry Bygren 1, Campbell 5, Lee Perrigo 7, Roger Seelye 20, Dan Spoon 3, Dave Brinkel 4.

No. 11: Laurel 74, Bozeman 48

Date: January 18, 1969; Location: Bozeman

Tom Perrigo, Roger Seelye and Jerry Bygren combined for 55 points as the Locomotives blasted Bozeman.

Perrigo poured in 19 points, and Seelye and Bygren tallied 18 each.

No scoring summary available.

No. 12: Laurel 70, Glendive 41

Date: January 24, 1969; Location: Laurel

Glendive held an early lead, but the Locomotives rallied, took control and romped.

The Red Devils grabbed an 11-5 advantage with about five minutes gone in the first quarter. Laurel, though, pulled into a 14-all tie at the end of the period, held the halftime lead, 32-24, and widened its advantage to 49-29 entering the fourth quarter.

Tom Perrigo, who came into the game averaging 20.2 points per contest, paced the Locomotives with 21 points. Teammates who reached double figures included Alan Campbell, 14 points; Jerry Bygren 11; and Roger Seelye, 10.

Laurel scoring summary: Tom Perrigo 21, Roger Seelye 10, Alan Campbell 14, Jerry Bygren 11, Lee Perrigo 3, Dave Brinkel 3, Mike Belinak 1, Ric Peterson 2, Clint Rooley 2, Gerry Ready 2, Miller 1.

No. 13: Laurel 81, Sidney 60

Date: January 25, 1969; Location: Laurel

Every piston pounded out power as the Locomotives rolled to a comfortable win over the Eagles. Eleven Laurel players scored, four reaching double figures, and the home team outrebounded the visitors, 62-33.

Tom Perrigo led the way with 17 rebounds and 14 points. Alan Campbell followed with 16 points, Roger Seelye chipped in 12, and Jerry Bygren added 11.

Laurel scoring summary: Tom Perrigo 14, Roger Seelye 12, Jerry Bygren 11, Alan Campbell 16, Lee Perrigo 4, Mark Metzger 8, Leon Schmidt 5, Dave Brinkel 2, Mike Belinak 1, Rick Peterson 4, Gerry Ready 4.

No. 14: Laurel 56, Lewistown 53

Date: January 31, 1969; Location: Lewistown

Laurel upheld its newly attained No. 2 state power poll ranking with a gritty, come-from-behind on the road.

The Locomotives erased an eight-point Golden Eagles lead in the fourth quarter. It was, Laurel players agreed as they looked back years later, one of their two most challenging regular-season games, the other being a one-point win over Billings Senior at the Broncs' gym in December 1968.

To keep their streak alive, the Locomotives turned to Tom Perrigo and Alan Campbell in the fourth quarter. The senior forward and senior guard combined for 12 of Laurel's 16 points in the frame.

Laurel forged a 15-8 first-quarter lead, but the Eagles rallied to tie the game at halftime, 28-all. The teams stayed tied at 37-all after three quarters.

Campbell, who had been averaging 15 points a game, scored 19. Perrigo, who brought a 19.8-point scoring average, tallied 16.

Laurel scoring summary: Alan Campbell 19, Tom Perrigo 16, Roger Seelye 16, Jerry Bygren 6, Mark Metzger 4, Leon Schmidt 1.

February 1969

No. 15: Laurel 65, Livingston 54

Date: February 1, 1969; Location: Laurel

Senior forward Tom Perrigo scored a season-high 28 points, powering the Locomotives to an easy win over the Rangers.

Laurel led at all the quarter stops, 17-11, 38-26, and 48-39. With his team up by 15 points in the fourth quarter, Locomotives coach Don Peterson went to his bench and gave reserves ample playing time.

Alan Campbell added 11 points to the winning total.

Laurel scoring summary: Tom Perrigo 28, Roger Seelye 5, Jerry Bygren 4, Alan Campbell 11, Mark Metzger 4, Lee Perrigo 5, Leon Schmidt 4, Dave Brinkel 2, Dan Spoon 2.

No. 16: Laurel 74, Billings Central 64

Date: February 7, 1969; Location: Laurel

The Locomotives held off the hot-shooting Rams, who got within four points of Laurel in the fourth quarter but couldn't close the gap.

The win almost assured the Locomotives of the No. 1 ranking in the state power poll because Great Falls Russell upset top-ranked (and defending state Big 32 champion) Wolf Point.

Laurel shook off an early 9-3 deficit to take a 22-15 first-quarter lead. The Locomotives lead grew to 42-32 at halftime, but the Rams refused to fold. They closed the gap to eight points, 58-50, after three quarters and whittled Laurel's lead down to four points, 60-56, with 6:13 left in the game.

With his team leading, 66-60, Laurel's Tom Perrigo sealed the outcome by scoring a driving layup and adding two free throws to give the Locomotives a 70-60 lead with more than two minutes left in the game.

Although Central's box-and-one zone defense focused on Perrigo, the smooth forward took game honors with 23 points. Jerry Bygren tallied 17 points, and Alan Campbell added 13.

Campbell and Perrigo sparked Laurel's ball-hawking defense, which came up with 22 turnovers compared with 13 given up by the Locomotives. Laurel also controlled the boards, finishing with a 51-29 edge.

Central, however, found the range, both at the free-throw line (20-of-23 conversion, compared with Laurel's 26-of-38) and from the field (51 percent, compared with Laurel's 38 percent).

Laurel scoring summary: Lee Perrigo 9, Tom Perrigo 23, Campbell 13, Roger Seelye 8, Jerry Bygren 17, Leon Schmidt 2, Mark Metzger 2.

No. 17: Laurel 68, Bozeman 47

Date: February 8, 1969; Location: Laurel

The Locomotives cruised past the Hawks, piling up quarter leads of 21-8, 34-20, and 52-31. Laurel's lead bulged to 28 points in the third quarter, prompting coach Don Peterson to send in reserves to finish the game.

Leon Schmidt took scoring honors for Laurel with 13 points. Tom Perrigo, averaging more than 20 points a game and the Locomotives' leading scorer, scored 12 points while playing only the first half. Other double-figure scorers were Alan Campbell (12) and Roger Seelye (10). Jerry Bygren, a stalwart of Laurel's front line, made a brief appearance after suffering an ankle injury in the game the night before.

Laurel scoring summary: Tom Perrigo 12, Roger Seelye 10, Alan Campbell 12, Lee Perrigo 7, Leon Schmidt 13, Dave Brinkel 5, Dan Spoon 4, Gerry Ready 5.

No. 18: Laurel 59, Miles City 53

Date: February 14, 1969; Location: Miles City

Sporting a No. 1 ranking in the state power poll, the Locomotives held off the Cowboys in a rugged contest.

Miles City was called for 17 fouls, compared with Laurel's nine.

Alan Campbell and Tom Perrigo paced the Locomotives, scoring 23 points and 20 points.

Laurel scoring summary: Tom Perrigo 20, Jerry Bygren 6, Leon Schmidt 2, Alan Campbell 23, Lee Perrigo 2, Roger Seelye 6.

No. 19: Laurel 61, Livingston 50

Date: February 20, 1969; Location: Livingston

The Locomotives held off the surprisingly competitive Rangers in a game that wasn't decided until halfway through the fourth quarter.

Livingston took a 16-15 first-quarter lead, but Laurel surged ahead, 30-28, at halftime and maintained the same margin with a 38-36 advantage after three quarters.

Alan Campbell sealed the win four minutes into the fourth quarter. He scored on a fast break to give the Locomotives a 49-41 lead.

Campbell and Tom Perrigo, building their credentials for all-state honors, paced Laurel with 22 points and 21 points, respectively.

Laurel scoring summary: Dan Spoon 2, Campbell 22, Lee Perrigo 2, Jerry Bygren 7, Tom Perrigo 21, Roger Seelye 5.

No. 20: Laurel 71, Billings Central 62

Date: February 22, 1969; Location: Billings West High School gym

The Locomotives gained Big 32 elite status and a place in Treasure State basketball history by holding off the arch-rival Rams in a regular-season finale played before a standing-room-only crowd of 3,100 at the West High gym. The contest, a home game for Central, was moved across town to the larger facility to accommodate high fan interest.

With the win, Laurel became the first Class AA-A team in five years – since the inaugural Big 32 season – to finish regular-season play undefeated. The only other team to do so was Mike Lewis-led Missoula High School in 1964, which won the state championship with its 49th consecutive win. Missoula extended its state-record boys basketball win streak to 56 games the following season.

The Locomotives weren't lacking for star power of their own during this season – or in this game. Forward Roger Seelye poured in 22 points, Tom Perrigo tossed in 17 during the first half, and Jerry Bygren tallied 15.

Perrigo was often double-teamed but was virtually unstoppable. He got in foul trouble in the second half, however, and fouled out with 5:22 remaining without scoring in the half.

Deadly free-throw shooting helped the Locomotives end up winners. They converted 17 of 19 free-throw attempts in the second half and 23 of 29 for the game, compared with Central's 13 of 23.

The Rams closed within eight points early in the fourth quarter before the Locomotives' disciplined offense and Central's troubles at the free throw line proved critical. Laurel built a 16-point lead, 66-50, with 2:49 left. The Locomotives used reserves down the stretch, which allowed the Rams to narrow the margin to the final score.

The game was a personal triumph for guard Alan Campbell. He earned all-state honors at Billings Central as a junior before deciding to transfer to Laurel for his senior year – a decision that prompted heckling from some Central fans.

Laurel scoring summary: Alan Campbell 5, Lee Perrigo 6, Jerry Bygren 15, Tom Perrigo 17, Roger Seelye 22, Dave Brinkel 2, Leon Schmidt 2.

Tournament play (March 1969)

Division 1 – Great Falls

No. 21: Laurel 80, Great Falls Central 49

Date: February 27, 1969

Alan Campbell's spectacular play led the Locomotives past the Mustangs and into the divisional tournament semifinals.

Campbell, a senior guard gaining the eye of college recruiters with his quickness and precision passing, broke free for five layups en route to a game-high 20 points. Three other Locomotives reached double figures: Jerry Bygren, 17 points; Tom Perrigo, 16; and sub Dan Spoon, 11.

The Mustangs initially proved more competitive than expected. They led most of the first quarter before settling for a 14-all tie at the buzzer. Their threat ended, however, with a tie at 19, after which the Locomotives reeled off 17 points to grab a 36-19 lead.

Spoon's scoring drive gave Laurel its biggest lead of the first half, 40-21. Ahead 40-25 at intermission, the Locomotives pulled away to a 67-39 advantage after three quarters.

Laurel's full-court press bothered the Mustangs, forcing costly turnovers.

The Locomotives ended with an edge in field goals, 29 to their opponents' 17, and free throws, 22 converted in 30 tries compared with 15 of 28 for the Mustangs.

The win advanced the Locomotives to the semifinals against Lewistown, which knocked off Great Falls in a first-round game.

Laurel scoring summary: Alan Campbell 20, Roger Seelye 5, Lee Perrigo 3, Jerry Bygren 17, Tom Perrigo 16, Gerry Ready 2, Spoon 11, Dave Brinkel 2.

No. 22: Laurel 66, Lewistown 48

Date: February 28, 1969

Laurel's rugged defense resulted in key steals, and outstanding offensive play and rebounding sealed the Locomotives' semifinal win over the Golden Eagles.

Laurel led at all quarter stops, 18-8, 36-15, and 48-30.

Roger Seelye paced Laurel with 20 points, Jerry Bygren added 15, and Tom Perrigo tallied 13. Alan Campbell, normally a double-figure scorer, concentrated on passing and defense. He scored nine points.

Laurel scoring summary: Lee Perrigo 5, Alan Campbell 9, Roger Seelye 20, Tom Perrigo 13, Bygren 15, Leon Schmidt 2, Rick Peterson 2.

No. 23: Laurel 52, Great Falls Russell 47 (divisional championship)

Date: March 1, 1969

The Locomotives seemed set to make the title game a cakewalk, but the Rustlers had other ideas. Behind by as much as 19 points in the first half, Russell twice closed to within three points in the fourth quarter before sophomore Gerry Ready and reserve Dan Spoon kept Laurel's win streak alive.

The contest, played before a turn away crowd of 5,500 spectators, belonged to the Locomotives early. They led, 22-8, after the first quarter and increased their margin to 19, 31-12, on Alan Campbell's bucket with 2:10 left in the first half. Laurel held a 33-17 edge at intermission.

Campbell's reverse layup in the third quarter gave Laurel a 39-22 lead, and the Locomotives owned a 45-34 advantage starting the fourth quarter.

The fourth quarter, however, turned tense for the Locomotives. Cousins Lee and Tom Perrigo, and Jerry Bygren, all starters, fouled out. Russell also lost center Larry Landsverk to fouls in the third quarter.

Laurel claimed the title thanks to the clutch play of two reserves who were not usually in the spotlight. Ready, the only non-senior on the team, sank two free throws, and Dan Spoon scored a field goal and two free throws to give the Locomotives breathing room.

Campbell took game scoring honors with 20 points on a variety of shots. Spoon added 11.

Laurel made 17 field goals and went 18-for-33 at the free throw line. Russell nearly mirrored that, sinking 16 field goals and 15 of 29 free throws. The Locomotives were whistled for 26 fouls, the Rustlers for 25.

Laurel scoring summary: L. Perrigo 6, T. Perrigo 8, Campbell 20, Ready 2, Bygren 2, Roger Seelye 2, Spoon 11, Leon Schmidt 1.

State Tournament

Bozeman

Montana State University Fieldhouse

No. 24: Laurel 71, Missoula Hellgate 47

Date: March 13, 1969

The Locomotives hit an astounding 35 of 45 free throws and rallied from a first-quarter deficit to romp over the Knights and reach the state tournament semifinal round.

Hellgate took an early 8-0 lead and was still ahead, 12-4, in the opening period before Laurel found its footing. Trailing 14-9 at the end of the first quarter, the Locomotives used Tom Perrigo's three-point play at 2:36 of the second quarter to go ahead for good.

Laurel built a 26-23 halftime lead and dominated the second half behind the rebounding of Perrigo and fellow senior Jerry Bygren.

Laurel set a Big 32 state tournament record for free throws made, and the total free throws made by both teams (50) equaled a mark set the year before.

The Locomotives' 48-30 lead at the end of the third quarter allowed coach Don Peterson to play reserves much of the fourth quarter.

Meanwhile, Butte Central upset defending state champion Wolf Point, 46-40, in another first-round game. That assured a new Big 32 champion for all six years of the league's existence. The Maroons' win also erased the possibility of a Big 32 dream matchup that many prep basketball observers around the Treasure State had been hoping for: the 1968 Cinderella championship team, Wolf Point from the Class A ranks, versus Laurel, also from Class A, which defeated larger schools in Hoosiers-like fashion.

No. 25: Laurel 63, Butte Central 56

Date: March 14, 1969

The Locomotives advanced to their first-ever state basketball championship game by holding off the Maroons in front of the biggest crowd to ever watch a basketball game in Montana.

Senior guard Alan Campbell's playmaking ability and the spark his steals provided to Laurel's pressure defense proved the difference in the close contest.

An overflow crowd of 10,700 spectators poured into the Montana State University Fieldhouse. The attendance surpassed the previous record of 10,200 set in 1958 – the fieldhouse's first season – when Seattle University played then-Montana State College. That game gave Montanans a chance to see future NBA star Elgin Baylor, who as a junior that year led Seattle to the NCAA championship game, where the Chieftains (now Redhawks) lost to Kentucky.

The Locomotives triumphed against the Maroons in spite of having two ailing starters. Senior center Jerry Bygren was battling strep throat, and senior forward Tom Perrigo had flu-like symptoms.

Laurel's path to victory became more challenging in the second half when Bygren and Perrigo, the squad's tallest players at 6-foot-2, were benched with four fouls each. Campbell and Roger Seelye, however, stepped up. Campbell tossed in 17 points, while Seelye contributed 15 points and 11 rebounds.

The Locomotives also got another clutch performance from sophomore Gerry Ready, the lone non-senior on the squad. Ready, who started the season as a junior varsity player but was pulled up to the varsity earlier in the winter, hit two free throws with 14 seconds left to ice the win. He added two free throws at the buzzer.

Central led, 12-10, at the end of the first quarter, but Laurel surged ahead, 32-23, at halftime. The Locomotives owned a 43-34 margin as the third quarter ended.

Both teams made 47 percent of their field goal attempts, but Laurel won the game at the free-throw line, converting 23 of 35 attempts to Central's 16-for-22 shooting.

No. 26: Laurel 57, Flathead of Kalispell 54 (Overtime)

Date: March 15, 1969

Once again, a Montana-record (for basketball games of either gender, at any level of play) crowd of 10,700 streamed into the Montana State University Fieldhouse. Another 500 fans (estimated) were turned away at the door; some of them listened to the game broadcast statewide on KOOK radio station in Billings while parked in the fieldhouse lot.

Whether watching in person or listening over the radio, thousands of Montanans experienced a classic championship game.

The Locomotives, who had no one taller than 6-2, more than held their own with the Braves, whose front line included 6-11 junior center Brent Wilson, 6-7 senior forward Don Groven and 6-4 senior forward Greg Ellingson.

Adding to the Hoosiers-like atmosphere, Laurel's enrollment at the start of the school year, 431 students, made it the 28th smallest of the 32 schools in the combined Class AA/A (Big 32) league. Kalispell's enrollment, officially 1,378, was more than three times larger, and some who were Kalispell students at the time have said they thought the actual enrollment approached 1,600 or perhaps even 1,700 students.

The outcome revolved around the final 6½ minutes – 3:30 of regulation play plus the three-minute overtime period.

Senior center Jerry Bygren, one of Laurel's 6-2 players, made two free throws early in the extra period to put the Locomotives ahead for good, 55-53. An Ellingson free throw made it 55-54.

Lee Perrigo clinched Laurel's first state championship. The 5-8 senior dribbled the ball, helping the Locomotives work their four-corner offense in the final minute, and then saw a lane to the hoop.

He swooped in for a layup, making it 57-54 and punctuating the victory.

Laurel led 45-37 starting the fourth quarter, a mirror image of the Locomotives' eight-point deficit in the first half. The Braves, however, rallied behind the play of Wilson and Groven, who returned to play after being benched by coach Paul Gologoski when each collected his fourth foul in the third quarter.

Groven sank a short jumper to make it 51-all with 3:25 left. Laurel answered, Alan Campbell converting a one-and-one for a 53-51 lead.

Campbell, who would earn all-state honors for the second year in a row (as a junior, he played for Billings Central), got a chance to pad the Locomotives' lead but missed the front of a one-and-one.

Laurel missed another opportunity a few moments later. Groven fouled out, sending Tom Perrigo to the line but he missed the first shot of a one-and-one.

A Wilson layup tied the game at 53 with 1:50 left in regulation.

There the score stayed, although both teams missed chances to win late in the fourth quarter. First, Wilson threaded a pass to Ellingson, open beneath the basket, but he bobbled the ball out of bounds going in for a layup. Then, Wilson fouled out with two seconds left. That sent Tom Perrigo to the line, but he missed the first shot of a one-and-one, sending the game into overtime.

Campbell led all scorers with 19 points. Groven and Wilson paced Kalispell with 17 points/13 rebounds and 14 points/12 rebounds.

Kalispell outshot Laurel from the field, 42 percent to 36 percent. The Locomotives compensated at the free-throw line where they went 15-for-29, compared with the Braves' 10-for-18.

APPENDIX B

Where are they now?

MIKE BELINAK

Mike graduated from Eastern Montana College (now Montana State University Billings) with an education degree. He taught math, physics and chemistry in three Montana high schools – Laurel, Park City and Huntley Project – and in Wyoming. He also ran a truss plant for six years. His longest employment was with the CHS Refinery in Laurel, a 26-year stint that ended with his retirement in 2014. His final position at the refinery was console operator. He and his wife, Barb, live in Laurel.

DAVE BRINKEL

Dave Brinkel has traveled farthest from his Laurel roots. A reserve on the 1969 team, he made golf course construction his life work – an understandable career choice since his father, Joe, was the first superintendent of the Laurel Golf Course when it opened in the late 1960s. As of 2014, Dave Brinkel was project director for a Donald Trump golf course being constructed in Dubai and scheduled for completion by Christmas that year. He said the course was designed by Gil Hanse, who also designed the layout for the 2016 Summer Olympics in Rio de Janeiro.

Interviewed via Skype, Brinkel described a path to the Gulf States nation that first took him, after high school graduation, to the

University of Montana, which he attended for two years. He worked in Denver a few years and moved back to Laurel, where he worked a while more. Next stop: Ennis, Montana, where he built and maintained the local golf course. Then it was on to Dickinson, N.D., for a three-year turn.

"I got a call from a guy I had met; he asked me if I was interested in working overseas. I told him I had never given it a thought, but three weeks later, I was on a plane," Brinkel said.

He lived eight years in Europe, working in Germany, Austria and Spain and also handling projects in the Caribbean. A stint in Jamaica, where he was involved in preparations for a golf tournament, resulted in his living there for eight years. He also worked in Barbados and Florida before heading to Dubai, where he has worked for 12 years. Brinkel's wife and youngest daughter live in Florida. Their two older daughters live in Bozeman. They have a grandson.

JERRY BYGREN

Montana's Flathead area, the hub of which is Kalispell, Laurel's opponent in the 1969 state championship game, has long drawn one-time Wyoming youngster Jerry Bygren. After graduating from LHS, he returned to Flathead Lake Lodge in Bigfork to work for the Averill family before leaving for Concordia College in Moorhead, Minnesota, which he attended for two years on a partial basketball scholarship.

In 1972, he transferred to the University of Montana and was reunited with Locomotives teammate Tom Perrigo. He and several Wolf Point players, who had been part of powerhouse Wolves teams, joined forces as the "Loco Lobos" to compete in city league and intramural basketball. After earning a degree in accounting, Jerry went back to the Flathead. After a short stint as a realtor, he began a 41-year career (as of 2016) with Flathead Bank of Bigfork. He is president and a director of the bank.

Jerry has two sons, a daughter and two grandchildren from his first marriage. He remarried in 2005 during the National Finals Rodeo in Las Vegas. His wife, Sarah, retired as the high school art teacher in Bigfork, the same school where Laurel coach Don Peterson finished his coaching career and where Jerry served as his assistant. Sarah has two daughters and three grandchildren.

"We enjoy riding our horses and still team rope," he said in 2016. "We enjoy golf, traveling around the country and attending Griz football games. Living near Kalispell, I run into folks who also remember the '69 Big 32 championship game but do not share the same enthusiasm at the outcome as I have."

ALAN CAMPBELL

Alan Campbell and his wife, Bronwyn, live in the West Texas city of Merkel. He retired in 2015, after a 38-year teaching and coaching career that included stops in Montana – he was at Red Lodge, Laurel and Billings Central high schools – and Washington, Australia and Texas. In Merkel, the last place he taught after a stint in El Paso, Campbell served six years in local government on the city council, as mayor pro tempore, and on the economic development board. He still drives a bus for the local school district.

Campbell has two daughters and a granddaughter living in California. Two stepsons live in Texas.

Campbell earned a degree in secondary education from Eastern Montana College (now Montana State University Billings), but his path to those credentials was anything but straightforward. When he graduated from LHS, he had a choice of two athletic scholarships and could have gone to Utah. His father's failing health, however, prompted him to stay close to home in Billings. He enrolled at Rocky Mountain College but was only there a few days. A conversation with Jim Brandenburg, then starting the men's basketball program at Flathead Valley Community College, convinced him to join the new team in Kalispell.

Campbell said FVCC attracted several players who went on to NBA careers, even stardom. Their talent-laden roster allowed the Trappers to defeat everyone in the state, including the freshmen teams at the University of Montana and Montana State University, he said. FVCC averaged 99 points a game and defeated a Washington state juco, 169-69.

Brandenburg moved to UM as an assistant coach, and Campbell came back to Billings for another try at Rocky. UM then hired Jud Heathcote, whose Michael Ray Richardson-led Grizzlies pulled off a near upset of UCLA in the 1975 NCAA tournament; Heathcote later left Missoula to become coach at Michigan State, where his Magic Johnson-led Spartans captured the 1979 national championship. Campbell returned to Missoula and re-enrolled at UM, but Brandenburg left for the University of Wyoming – he coached San Diego State after that – and Campbell enrolled at EMC. After getting his degree, he headed to Australia to teach, and he also played semi-pro basketball. While Down Under, he had a surprise meeting with former Laurel teammate Tom Perrigo, who also was teaching in Australia. The two Locomotive stars didn't know they both were in the country until they bumped into each other in Melbourne.

MARK METZGER

Reserve guard Mark Metzger attended a vocational-technical school in Denver after high school graduation. He achieved his wish of working around cars, landing a job at the auto facility at the Burlington Northern Santa Fe railway yard in Laurel. This turned into 44 years of employment, as of 2016 – longer than anyone else at the facility.

Nowadays, Metzger runs his own business. He has a contract with BNSF to unload new vehicles and oversee delivery to dealerships throughout Montana and in North Dakota, South Dakota and Wyoming. "If you drive a Ford, a Honda or a Subaru, I probably drove it first," he said of his job.

LEE PERRIGO

After high school, Lee enrolled at Arizona State University. He attended ASU for three years and worked on campus for two years. He got married and landed a job at the Farmers Union Refinery (now CHS) in Laurel. Lee retired in 2013 after 37 years at the facility; his last job was console operator. He and his wife, Debby, have five children, 10 grandchildren, and one great-grandchild.

TOM PERRIGO

Former Montana State University coach Roger Craft recruited Tom to Bozeman as part of a crop of standout Montana high school basketball players in 1969. Craft's goal was to mold what might be called a Montana "dream team" capable of competing for regional and even national titles. Before Craft could get started, however, he and MSU parted ways. Perrigo played for MSU's freshmen team – NCAA rules required sophomore status for playing varsity basketball – but grew disillusioned with basketball and sports. He transferred to the University of Montana and earned a degree in education while adding science coursework.

An opportunity to teach in Western Australia lured him to the Island Continent. After teaching four years, he returned to Missoula and earned a master's degree associated with sciences and education. He went back to Australia. He and his wife, Lynn, an Australian woman to whom he has been married since 1977, lived on Rottnest Island, in the Indian Ocean off the coast of Western Australia, for eight years. He worked for a museum, in charge of environmental and education matters. Because their children were growing up, Tom and Lynn wanted to assure they wouldn't have to go to boarding school on the mainland, so he searched for other work.

The National Trust of Australia hired Tom, and he became the organization's CEO in 1990. The National Trust, partly a charity and partly government-funded, is modeled after a like-named group in the United Kingdom. Australia's trust cares for heritage places in the "built" environment, the aboriginal environment and the natural environment. Tom's responsibility included managing more than 100 properties and thousands of natural environment pictures; he also interacted with eight aboriginal foundations. His work took him throughout Western Australia, a state of the country about equivalent in size to one-third of the United States.

Tom has lived in or near Perth almost continuously since 1975. He and his wife have three adult children and two grandchildren. Lynn Perrigo and his son have visited Laurel. Perrigo retired from the trust in November 2015 but continues as a consultant and has other consulting contracts in Australia.

RIC PETERSON

After high school, Ric attended Eastern Montana College and worked seasonally in Yellowstone National Park. He joined the United States Air Force and trained as a field medic and ophthalmic tech. He married Cindy Robbins in 1976 and they moved to Oregon where he attended Pacific University and received an optometry degree. He returned to active duty in the Air Force, alternating between clinical duty and research assignments.

Basketball remained a major part of Peterson's life; he played on and coached five military league championship teams during a career spanning more than 36 years. He picked up coaching counsel from his father, Don Peterson, through phone calls most Sunday nights until the former Locomotives coach died in 2003.

Ric retired in 2003. He and his wife live in the Dallas area, where he still practices optometry. They have two daughters and a son and three grandsons.

GERRY READY

After getting an education degree from Rocky Mountain College in Billings, Gerry taught for two years in Fromberg and then returned to Laurel. He taught six years in his hometown and served as a freshman basketball coach at the high school one year while teammate Alan Campbell coached the varsity squad. He also coached basketball five years in the Laurel middle school. Gerry left education to work at the CHS refinery, from which he retired at the end of 2015, ending a 30-year turn. His jobs at the facility included operations, involved in petroleum processing; the machine shop, repairing pumps and compressors, the instrumentation shop, working with electrical equipment; the laboratory; and his final job, in the warehouse, receiving and inventory. He and his wife, Bonnie, have three children.

CLINT ROOLEY

Rooley, a reserve guard during the 1968-69 season, lives in East Canton, Ohio, where he is a transportation consultant. After high school, he earned a psychology degree from Montana State University and a master's degree from the University of Guelph in Ontario. He worked as a research associate at the University of Denver and then became an executive with transportation software companies and manufacturing firms based in Montana, Indiana, New Jersey and Ontario.

LEON SCHMIDT

After high school, Leon went to a trade school and came back to Billings, where he worked for Deluxe Check Printing. That company's consolidation resulted in his being transferred to Salt Lake City, where Leon worked for 20-plus years.

After 44 years of working for Deluxe, Leon retired in 2015. He and his wife, both Laurel natives, returned to their hometown. Nowadays, Leon drives a school bus for the Laurel district, driving school routes and extracurricular activity trips

He and his wife, Deborah, have three daughters and two granddaughters.

ROGER SEELYE

Roger Seelye, who played alongside Tom Perrigo to give Laurel a pair of forwards as polished as any in the state during the championship season, is a longtime resident of Lancaster, California. He attended the University of Montana for a couple years and then became a construction supervisor for Motel Six. The economy chain was expanding across the U.S., and Seelye went along for the ride. The job took him all over the country for three years, but he said he tired of living in motels and moved back to Laurel.

A colleague living in California called to ask if he was interested in working there. It was mid-winter in Montana, and Seelye realized he could work 365 days a year in the construction industry in southern California, so he moved to Lancaster and has been a resident there since 1978.

Besides building motels, his career experience includes construction of schools, prisons, military facilities and a variety of commercial projects.

Even in Lancaster, Seelye retains a strong personal connection to Laurel through his wife, the former Sheri Muri. He and Sheri, a cheerleader for LHS in 1969 and a track star for the Locomotives, dated in high school. About 40 years later, they reconnected and married. In an email, Sheri said she and Roger enjoy excursions on their Lake Mead houseboat, trailer camping, and "keeping up with (our) combined kids and grandkids."

DAN SPOON

Dan took followed an indirect path to college and his current profession as a lawyer. Facing the likelihood of being drafted and sent into combat in Vietnam after high school graduation, Spoon enlisted in the Air Force. He was sent to a base in England where he was a Morse Code interceptor.

"I was a spy. ... The Russians would fly from Moscow to Cuba. They'd do their Morse Code, and we would track them. It was kind of ridiculous," he said.

After discharge, Spoon earned a degree in business and a law degree, both from the University of Montana. He owns a law firm in Missoula and also owns a pair of Montana businesses: a bed-and-breakfast and ranch in Phillips and a ranch near Townsend.

Spoon worked at one time in Great Falls. He put up a notice saying he wanted to play city league basketball. He said he got three calls from individuals asking, "Are you the Dan Spoon from Laurel, the undefeated (team)?

"There's a lot of people who relate to that team. I've talked to hundreds of people (who were at the MSU Fieldhouse on March 15, 1969) and saw that game. It's a piece of legend in Montana history," he said.

Spoon's daughter and son were both standout basketball players at Missoula Sentinel High School.

Afterword

1969 was a much different time than now, and when one reads this book today, there may be a tendency to assume it is a snapshot in time about a bunch of boys led by a brilliant coach and supported by a group of very dedicated people - coaches, managers, cheerleaders, parents and friends achieving success. In a way, this is true and no doubt the reader will enjoy a traditional story of David vs Goliath – how Laurel became the permanent home of the Big 32 trophy.

However, the real story is how sport shapes a path for those who are both directly involved and those who take part as supporters. It is about how sport, for a moment in time, can bring together a community in a small town in Montana in a challenging era and despite all the differences between individuals, they celebrated and continue to celebrate with great pride an experience shared by all. Within this moment in time, values were created and stamped on the souls of all those involved and continue to play a substantial part in their lives. This is in true for the players in this story and the author.

This scenario is one which has been repeated throughout time and whether it is a Super Bowl championship or an Olympic gold medal, the story is the same.

Those who were lucky enough to be part of the experience in Laurel in 1969 can no doubt look back and, in their own way, reflect on the impact the experiences had on their lives.

As players, we were taught the importance of teamwork, of learning that an assist is as valuable as a basket and rebounds were to be an obsession. Most of all, we were taught about systems and persistence, and whatever we needed to do relied on the training that was instilled in our minds. We also learned about the values and the power of a community's spirit.

At first glance, winning a high school championship in Montana may not appear to be a story with obvious appeal outside a state that still registers a blank look with many people. Yet, this is a quintessential All-American story that will resonate with people who love sport in a way that is sometimes forgotten in an era of spoiled professional athletes and megabucks TV contracts for rights to broadcast over-hyped games.

Through this book, many of us have had the opportunity to reflect and be very thankful for being a part of the community in Laurel in 1969. That is something no one can ever take away. How lucky we have been to be Montana Champions!

Tom Perrigo
Co-Captain of the 1969 Cinderstellar Locomotives
Perth, Australia
April 2016

Photos from the Cinderstellar season

Please note: all pictures reproduced in this book, except those credited to the author, were scanned from snapshots (photos taken by Laurel Leaves photographers) or captured from microfilm (photos taken by Billings Gazette photographers). Negatives , which provide higher quality, no longer exist. Thus, these archival photos do not meet normal book-publishing quality standards. Yet, for historical purposes, it was important to include them.

The MSU Fieldhouse, as it appeared when the arena opened in 1958. Hosting college rodeos was a primary purpose for the facility; hence, the hardwood floor for basketball was placed above the dirt floor, with walkways to get on the court. (MSU Library Digital Archive Collection)

The Laurel Locomotives warm up to "Sweet Georgia Brown" before the 1969 title game (Jim Scott-*Laurel Leaves*).

Lee Perrigo (24), Laurel's 5-8 guard and the shortest player on the court, jumps center against Brent Wilson, Kalispell's 6-11 center and the tallest player in the game, to open the 1969 Big 32 championship clash. (Jim Scott-*Laurel Leaves*)

Billings Gazette photographer Bob Nunley used a fisheye lens to capture state Big 32 tournament action in the 1969 event in Bozeman. Nunley was part of a *Gazette* team covering the team that included Norm Clarke, sports editor; Addison Bragg, columnist and reporter; and Dennis Gaub, part-time sportswriter. (Photograph courtesy of the *Billings Gazette*. Used with permission.)

(Above) Lee Perrigo shoots against Brent Wilson in the championship game. (Jim Scott – *Laurel Leaves*). Laurel's Jerry Bygren, who was battling strep throat, comes down with a crucial rebound late in the state championship game. (Photograph courtesy of the *Billings Gazette*. Used with permission.)

Roger Seelye soars to shoot against Missoula Hellgate in the first game of the 1969 State Big 32 basketball tournament. (Photograph courtesy of the *Billings Gazette.* Used with permission.)

Laurel fans, who may have comprised one-fourth or more of the almost 11,000 spectators, are on pins and needles as the championship game winds down. (Jim Scott – *Laurel Leaves*)

The state champion Locomotives collect the winner's hardware (*Laurel Leaves* – Jim Scott)

The champion Locomotives return home to a jubilant welcome at the school parking lot. (Photograph courtesy of the *Billings Gazette*. Used with permission.)

Laurel's Roger Seelye goes for two against Great Falls Russell in the 1969 Division One tournament. (Jim Scott – *Laurel Leaves*)

Jerry Bygren shoots against Lewistown in Division One tournament play. (Jim Scott – *Laurel Leaves*).

Dan Spoon drives against Great Falls Russell during divisional tournament play. (Jim Scott – *Laurel Leaves*).

Jerry Bygren (34) jostles for the ball in Laurel's state tournament win over Butte Central, while teammate Alan Campbell (14) and Central's Dan Mahoney (22) await the outcome. (Jim Scott – *Laurel Leaves*)

(Above) Workers from the Continental Oil Refinery in Billings, along with those from the Humble Oil Refinery in Billings and the Laurel Farmers Union Refinery, joined a nationwide strike in January 1969. (Photograph courtesy of the *Billings Gazette*. Used with permission).
(Left) Dick Hatfield carried out an innovative strategy at the time: filming Laurel opponents to help scout their strengths and weaknesses. (Dennis Gaub)

(Top) Laurel Locomotives are jubilant after winning the 2015 state Class A championship on the same floor as their 1969 predecessors. (Dennis Gaub). (Bottom) Brick Breeden Fieldhouse in 2015. (Dennis Gaub)

Next

Get the scoop on books in progress by the author. Details below.

If you enjoyed "Win 'Em All," you may be interested in the author's next book, scheduled for release later in 2017. "Basketball break – High school hoops rally Montanans during the Great Depression, world war and a mine disaster," tells the story of another colorful era in Treasure State high school basketball history. That was from 1934-1946, when the state's high schools competed in two classes, big school (Class A) and all the rest (Class B). At the end of the season, the two top teams from each class (originally; later, top four) met in a round-robin tournament to decide Montana's all-state champion. Small schools did well – they won eight tournament games in that period – and their ranks included a pair of unforgettable squads, both from now all-but-deserted coal mining camps.

In 1939, Bearcreek High School tied big-school champ Livingston for the state title; four years later, the town of Bearcreek suffered the Smith Mine disaster, which killed 74 underground miners in Montana's worst coal mining accident. The February 1943 accident overwhelmed Bearcreek, and its high school, the social center, lost so many students it closed in 1950. In 1942, Klein reached the championship against Billings, which had about 40 times the population of the smaller town. Billings won, but the game produced a direct connection to the 1969 state championship. A son of one Klein's star players and a son of one of Billings' star players were teammates on the Laurel Locomotives squad that won the final Big 32 championship. And there are more stories to tell, within that story.

To stay in the loop on this book, sign up for email and a newsletter at treasure-state-heritage.dennisgaub.me

Another book in progress will tell the true story of a remarkable aviation feat on June 4, 1942, the opening day of the Battle of Midway, a pivotal event in World War II. During the early hours of that battle, which shifted the tide of combat in the Pacific from Japan to the United States, a pilot from Miles City, Montana, helped confuse and unnerve the Japanese command enough that carriers from nearby U.S. Carriers could swoop in and sink several Japanese ships -- part of the largest fleet in world history. The pilot of this B-26 Martin Marauder and the commander of their squadron of B-26s, Jim Collins, were the only pilots of four planes that had taken off from Midway Island able to bring their airplanes back safely to Midway after the encounter with the Japanese navy. Deadly anti-aircraft fire caused the loss of the other two planes and their crews lost at sea.

Fortunately for Muri, most guns on the ship were pointed out to sea and away from him. Still, as he flew away, Japanese Zeroes unleashed a barrage of cannon fire towards his plane. Somehow, Muri and his five-man crew evaded the attackers and eventually located Midway Island, the speck of land in the Pacific Ocean they needed for refuge. Muri crash-landed his B-26, nicknamed the Suzy Q for his wife of six months on Midway. When he and his crew got out, they counted bullet holes in the Marauder. They stopped at 500. The plane was scrapped and never flew again.

Historians now say Muri and Collins sowed confusion in the Japanese command: should they send more bombers to continue the attack on Midway begun early in the morning on June 4, or send bombers and fighters to find and attack the U.S. carriers the Japanese believed to be lurking somewhere beyond Midway? This was the prize that had eluded Japan in its December 7, 1941 attack on Pearl Harbor. This indecision allowed time for planes from those U.S. carriers to swoop in on the Japanese fleet, sink several ships and force Nagumo to make a U-turn and return to his base.

If you want to get updates on the progress of these books, sign up for email and a newsletter at: treasure-state-heritage.dennisgaub.me. You won't be bombarded with emails nor will your email address be shared. As a bonus, look for occasional "extras," items that won't get into the book, to show up in your inbox.

ABOUT THE AUTHOR

Author Dennis Gaub was born in and grew up in in Montana. He left to receive a bachelor's degree in journalism from Northwestern University and began a newspaper reporting career that took him to Colorado, Wyoming and Michigan. He returned home and worked 20 years as a sportswriter and City Hall reporter for the Treasure State's largest newspaper, the Billings Gazette. He changed careers and worked in the software industry more than a decade. He is now a semi-retired bus driver in Bozeman, Montana. As a high school senior, working part-time for the Gazette, Dennis helped cover the dramatic climax of the story described here. He, his wife, Carolyn, and their son, Julian, a college sophomore, live in Belgrade, Montana – 20 minutes from where the Laurel Locomotives won the 1969 championship in unforgettable fashion.

CPSIA information can be obtained
at www.ICGtesting.com
Printed in the USA
FSHW04n0715110418
46832FS

9 781532 819803